T0386609

Building Successful Extracurricular Enrichment Programs

Building Successful Extracurricular Enrichment Programs is a must-read for educators or administrators who want to develop, implement and maintain engaging out-of-school programs.

Accessible and easy to use, the book focuses on four basic approaches to building enrichment programs: grassroots, semi-structured, franchise and fully structured. Readers will walk through each stage of the process, from conception to fundraising, to implementation and evaluation. Successful programs require significant time, energy and resources; this book makes what is often a very demanding process understandable and obtainable.

With practical tools and tips to support every student, this essential guidebook equips teachers, administrators and home educators with step-by-step strategies to confidently design their own extracurricular programs.

Michael Cain is a recently retired teacher with a career spanning 34 years. He has created over half a dozen successful afterschool and summer programs. Throughout his career, Cain has received various awards and accommodations. A mathematics instructor with a degree in fine art, Cain has incorporated his skills and talents to develop and implement educational enrichment throughout his community.

Building Successful Extracurricular Enrichment Programs

The Essential How-To Guide for Schools and Communities

Michael Cain

Routledge
Taylor & Francis Group

NEW YORK AND LONDON

First published 2022
by Routledge
605 Third Avenue, New York, NY 10158

and by Routledge
4 Park Square, Milton Park, Abingdon, Oxon, OX14 4RN

Routledge is an imprint of the Taylor & Francis Group, an informa business

Library of Congress Cataloging-in-Publication Data
A catalog record for this title has been requested

ISBN: 978-1-032-18515-6 (hbk)
ISBN: 978-1-032-18514-9 (pbk)
ISBN: 978-1-003-25491-1 (ebk)

DOI: 10.4324/9781003254911

Typeset in Palatino
by Deanta Global Publishing Services, Chennai, India

Contents

The Introduction
(or Don't Be Afraid)

There never is enough time in school to get all the experiences and information that we as teachers would like to impart to our students. Classes change and we need to often stop at a peak point in learning to accommodate a very crowded schedule. Every class is important, every experience needed, and yet, we don't have enough to fill the lives of our students with enrichment and the joy of learning new things or developing prior skills to a higher level. One of the best solutions available is the extracurricular enrichment program. The term itself extracurricular tells us that it's above and beyond what the day of learning provides. Enrichment tells us that whatever activity we're doing should bring something new and vital to the lives of the participants in the program. These two simple terms pull together, a larger purpose for us as educators. Most school curriculum is well-defined with the scope and sequence and often forces teachers to exclude topics that don't fit into the already crowded curriculum. My experience as a mathematics teacher often forced me to choose between a lesson I knew would be exciting and dynamic and the eligible content for high-stakes testing. It is hard to justify an enrichment topic when the fundamentals are so crucial to the students' test scores and a school's finances. Arguments can be made about how important certain enrichment topics are in every subject but the reality of high-stakes testing and the impact it has on everyone in the school district cannot be denied. Still, the need to enrich all of our students exists and the only alternative we have is to move to an extracurricular program. Stepping out beyond the school day for an educational and life experience that will enrich and provide needed skills and experiences for our students becomes a necessity.

Enrichment programs can take a variety of forms, from the most loosely structured to the most concrete and fully structured.

DOI: 10.4324/9781003254911-1

All of the enrichment programs I personally have been involved with had common components that can be easily replicated by other teachers interested in creating an extracurricular enrichment venue. This book is designed to be easily read and is filled with real experiences in creating these programs and a step-by-step methodology to help any interested parties in creating their own vibrant and dynamic extracurricular enrichment activities. My teaching experience spanned a period of 34 years. During that time, I initiated and took part in many successful extracurricular enrichment programs. Along the way, I had mentors that created dynamic programs outside the school day, and they provided me with vital information, role modeling and other examples to follow. My goal for this book is to inspire and guide prospective individuals that want to create positive life-changing educational experiences for their students.

The experiences that enrich students are the main objective of the types of extracurricular programs this book is designed to encourage. Students and their enrichment are at the center of what matters in creating these programs. Students' needs, desire to learn and enjoyment of education are paramount when it comes to creating extracurricular enrichment programs. Without students, these programs have no meaning. The most important reason for the program's existence is the enrichment of the student. All other purposes are secondary to the student. When the student is at the center of the program's purpose then the program will have true enrichment meaning. Meeting the needs of the student and enriching them is the primary purpose of these programs but not the sole purpose. A truly enriching experience impacts every individual involved in the program. When a program enriches every participant and staff member, it has accomplished its ultimate goal.

Throughout this book, the energy and effort necessary to create and maintain an enrichment program will not be downplayed. Successful programs require a lot of energy, time, and often, resources. This book hopes to guide individuals through what appears to be a very demanding process and makes it more understandable and obtainable. The demands on individuals that spearhead these programs are no greater than the demands of the head coach of an athletic team or any other type of administrative job. The demands are just different and do not exceed what is possible. Commitment and dedication are primary ingredients for these programs to succeed. When a program does succeed, the glorious impact it has on all lives can be realized and a sense of satisfaction of a job well done can come into being.

Throughout my teaching career, I have created a variety of different types of extracurricular enrichment programs. I define them by the amount of structure and how they come into being. These are my own definitions and concepts. I am not attached to the vocabulary of this book. Individuals can freely adapt the information to fit their needs. The terminologies I use will be discussed in this introduction for ease of understanding. The type of educational approach utilized throughout my career will center on constructivism and experiential learning. The main emphasis of the goals and products of the program will center around gaining new skills and refining previously acquired skills. The programs that I initiated, and what my mentors taught me, were all based on skills and their acquisition by students.

Within my first year of teaching, I had started an extracurricular enrichment program. My last and greatest success of a program came into being six years prior to my retirement. The extracurricular enrichment program has been part of my teaching career from the beginning to the end. I hope to share my knowledge and experiences with all interested parties in the hope that their students and faculty can benefit from my undertakings and develop even greater and more impactful and effective programs. I do not consider myself an expert on extracurricular enrichment programs but an experienced veteran willing to share knowledge of what to do and what not to do if a program is to be successful and maintainable. Each type of program I created will be examined and its components explored. The book's purpose is to make available to all individuals and organizations methods to help create enrichment programs that will positively impact the lives of the students and other participants in the program.

The term enrichment may have different meanings for different people and groups. Some type of a working definition that this book will use when referring to enrichment will be helpful. For the most part, the standard school day provides fundamentals on a variety of different disciplines. There are classes available that push beyond the fundamentals in some ways but still establish fundamental learning principles for the topic. Literature can expose students to higher-level writing and thinking skills when presented in a high school setting, but at a collegiate setting a more thorough and enriching approach becomes available. Had it not been for the fundamental exposure to these literary works and authors, post-secondary learning would suffer.

In mathematics, even at the calculus level, high school students may get advanced placement credit, but again, the true exploration into the mathematical theories that govern the operations of much of the mechanics of this world become more thoroughly examined at a collegiate level. Enrichment in the core subjects most often occurs in the post-secondary setting. For the purpose of this book, we are talking about high school, middle school and grade school students. Enrichment at these three levels takes different forms. The fundamental knowledge and skills the standard school day provide will make enrichment possible. Without fundamentals, enrichment would be very difficult if at all possible.

In K-12 enrichment, the fundamental skills are present and new applications and higher-order thinking take place to create enrichment. Just as the enrichment program is designed to take place outside of the standard school day, it also provides a deeper and more thorough investigation into topics and disciplines presented during the school day. The development of skills that are associated with fundamental disciplines and topics is at the very heart of enrichment programs. The application of knowledge and the expanding of experiences in which students can create their knowledge and understanding of a topic is the purpose of an enrichment program. The enrichment program can and should provide the "oh that's where you use this" answer to the question posed by many students. Often when teaching the fundamentals, it is hard to present the uses that are built upon those fundamentals. Enrichment programs need to expand knowledge developmental skills and be transformative in nature.

Wind turbines were the vehicle used in one of my programs to provide all three parts necessary for enrichment. The wind turbine will provide an example of how all three of these components can be incorporated in one enrichment activity. Students came with a basic knowledge of rotation, a circle, wind, electricity and energy. During the enrichment program, students were exposed to the concept of a wind turbine. They were given notes and their knowledge was expanded upon. Next, the students built their own operational scale models of a wind turbine. Once they had a working model, they had developed the skills to construct a wind turbine. With the use of LED lights and wiring, the challenge of lighting a scale model of a community was presented to the students. They were able to accomplish the lighting of the scale model community by utilizing all the skills and knowledge they had acquired experimenting with wind turbines. The students saw firsthand how alternative energy sources can create electricity. This experience transformed much of their thinking about the limitations of energy production. The students became enriched because their knowledge expanded, they developed new skills and it transformed their thinking.

The guidelines of expanded knowledge, skills and transformative thinking in enrichment programs can be built to make them successful and effective. Every program that I initiated and operated was based on these fundamentals. I did not initially know I was doing this when I first started working with extracurricular enrichment programs. It was upon reflection over a career and the writing of this book that I solidified my knowledge of how to create and operate enrichment programs. The very act of creating an enrichment program expanded my knowledge to increase my skills and it transformed my thinking. What I hope to do is share my successes and failures so that the challenge of creating such a magnificent program can be undertaken by any individual willing to put forth the time and effort.

Enrichment programs come in many sizes and forms. The four basic structures presented in this book are not the only structures available. The four basic structures were derived from my work, and I am sure that other people's work may have provided different structures that succeed in their purpose. The four basic structures that I utilized were a grassroots approach, a semi-structured approach, a franchise approach, and finally, a fully structured approach. All of these types of enrichment programs can be successful and effective. They can also fail miserably. This book should provide some warning signs of where a program can go astray and head into failure. Mainly, this book should provide a roadmap for any individual seeking to create these types of programs. The four varieties should give enough freedom for individuals to create their own style of enrichment program. It is my hope that after reading this book, individuals will develop a unique and successful enrichment program that fits the needs of the students.

Student enrichment is different from standard school day operations. In a standard school day, students are compelled if not conscripted to go to specific classes at specific times. An enrichment program is voluntary, whereas the standard school day may have some intrinsic motivation from students to learn, but it uses external motivation to maintain order and structure. Students follow the directions and procedures within the school because to deviate from them may result in adverse consequences. Students attend an enrichment program because they want to and have a desire to take part in its activities. There is a willingness to participate that may not be present in a standard school day. Therein lies the difference.

When I was teaching mathematics to high school students, whether they liked math or not, they had to attend my class and pass the course if they wanted that credit. In an extracurricular enrichment program, students attend because they have a desire for what the program has to offer and are connected by some personal motivation to learn and create. Achievements within a standard school day can be substantial, but in comparison to the achievements of a successful enrichment program, they will pale. Successful enrichment programs provide an overall experience that will impact their lives directly, whereas a class in a standard school day may provide only the experience of compliance and successfully completing an unpleasant task. The joy of learning is a significant part of any successful extracurricular enrichment program.

How these enrichment programs are formed have their similarities and their differences. They are all formed by student needs and a desire to learn. Some formations may be planned by educators and others by the students themselves, and still further, a combination of both can create an enrichment program. My first major extracurricular enrichment program utilized what I call the grassroots approach. Students lacked something to do after the school day had concluded. I worked late most days of the week. My classroom was comfortable and nonthreatening. Students began to gravitate to it after school to utilize the learning centers I had created and the resources available such as computers, markers, chalk and chalkboards boards and a variety of other materials. The students all had a common interest in creativity. Many of them wrote and drew pictures.

My experience prior to becoming a teacher was in the graphics art field. Seeing that I had half a dozen students willing to write and draw, we decided as a group to make a magazine. Word spread throughout the school about the afterschool magazine production and its freedom of creativity. Students' friends and other interested students joined the afterschool activity. The school administrators became aware of the significant number of students utilizing my classroom and materials to do positive creative work and were pleased and supportive. The students themselves were the motivation to create the program, henceforth, I refer to these types of programs as grassroots. Another type of program is the semi-structured program.

The semi-structured program has basic components common among all enrichment programs but it does not need to conform to the school's definition of a club or team. The semi-structured program has its rules that it follows. Rules that are in conjunction with general classroom operations, but it doesn't have the firm structure that a more established club such as a foreign language club would have. There are no elected officers and there is no fixed budget or financial component. Most often, the semi-structured programs come from a desire by the administration to fill a void in the afterschool activities of a group of students or the expansion of a classroom program. Skill acquisition, goals and products are the mainstays of all enrichment programs mentioned in this book.

Funding and resources are always at a premium for beginning and even established programs. Curriculum directors and other school administrators may be aware of larger educational initiatives and the availability of funding. They may be able to provide resources and the facilities necessary to conduct the program but lack the staffing to operate the program. An administrator can easily come to a teacher and ask if they would be interested in hosting the enrichment program and they may ease the burden of operations by handling the budget, providing resources and all the necessary materials for the program to operate successfully. What is required is a program director.

A program director is the term this book will use to describe an adult that facilitates enrichment activities and is key to creating the program. The semi-structured program allows the program director more freedom to be creative and more centered on student enrichment because a larger burden of administration has been taken off their shoulders. Though a grassroots program requires a teacher leader, a semi-structured and other forms of enrichment programs require the teacher leader to take on the mantle of program director.

A program director is a type of administrator. It is a very different type of administrator. The concepts of the extracurricular enrichment program expanded on in this book are based upon the leadership of one individual or a small group of individuals. Many stakeholders can be involved in the creation, funding and operation of enrichment programs but the buck has to stop somewhere. The program director holds a special spot. Someone has to steer the ship. The program director has the final say in decisions about the program. The program director is the ultimate person responsible for the operation of the enrichment activity. Becoming a program director is within the realm of possibilities for anyone who is interested and enthusiastically dedicated to an enrichment program. From start to finish, the program director is responsible for the overall functioning of this enrichment endeavor. The program director will be the key initiator of fundraising as well as the key initiator for the educational aspect of the program and all other components to make it a success-ful and viable enrichment event. The program director can be a single classroom teacher offering an enrichment program with a small group of students within their classroom or it can be an individual managing many instructors and other staff members. It is the program director's ultimate responsibility to see that every participant receives the full measure of enrichment that the program can provide.

Unlike other administrators that evaluate staff and enforce policies of a school district or organization, the program direc-tor is an ally to all and a servant to all and must have a differ-ent operating technique compared with other administrators. Remembering that an enrichment program involves voluntary participation by students and often staff, the program director walks a fine line of leadership and fellowship. The program direc-tor leads by example and is the first to arrive and the last to leave. The leadership demonstrated by a program director should be steady, compassionate and firm. The program director must be able to have a wide view of the goals of the program they are directing. The program director is a money manager and must be able to understand the financial aspects of the operation of the program. It is a complex and demanding job that is crucial in providing enriching skills experiences and transformative events that positively impact all the participants in the program. The program director must always have the vision of the program at the forefront of their mind.

From my experience in creating these extracurricular enrich-ment programs, two types of vision exist. I label them overall vision and operational vision. I utilized the concepts of these two visions in creating all of my programs. Though when I first started, I did not have the visions defined as clearly as I do now. The overall vision of a program is the main purpose for why there is a program. The overall vision should be a constant as the program develops and progresses. Making sure that each component of the program works in conjunction with the over-all vision will maintain the integrity of the program and add to the chances of success. An overall vision is a grand concept that involves the goals and products that should be produced or achieved by the enrichment program. Using a model building enrichment program is an example, an overall vision for it might be, "participants will learn the skills required in the construction of scale models, fine parts assembly and demonstrations." With an overall vision, a program can set its course, and if the vision can be maintained, it will achieve its purpose.

The next type of vision is the operational vision. The operational vision is a step-by-step process that each session of the program will follow. The operational vision can be vague and more open-ended than if it were a micromanaged event. Generalized activities and the time these activities will take up during the session need to be planned before the sessions begin. An operational vision allows for people involved with the program to explain what the program will be doing when it is in session. Both the overall vision and operational vision will be necessary for explaining the program to potential donors and other stakeholders in the program. Your operational vision is how you will achieve the goal of your overall vision. The more clearly the program director understands both types of visions the better they will be at acquiring the necessary funding and resources to operate the program at peak efficiency.

The ability to explain the goals and purposes of an extracurricular enrichment program directly impacts the capacity to acquire the funding necessary to operate the program. Potential donors and stakeholders need a clear understanding of what their investment will be doing for the children that are to be involved in the program. The more enthusiastic the presentation is the more likely support will be garnered. A lackluster presentation and vague vision of the program will not serve to entice potential stakeholders to participate or fund the endeavor. The more impacting the program is on the lives of the student participants, the higher the chance of gaining financial support and resources. Targeting the correct stakeholders for each type of program is also important. A connection with community service groups and other businesses in the community increases the probability that a new program will be supported. Potential program directors should work to connect with the community and the various organizations that are involved with the community. Funding will always be a problem. Asking for money can be stressful and can sometimes be unwelcome by the potential donor. Targeting interested parties is especially important and timing can be a major factor. Some organizations have a set time when they select what entities will be receiving donations. The complexities of fundraising cannot be overstated. It is just a fact that extracurricular programs often run very lean on finances. Sometimes a new program can piggyback onto a larger existing extracurricular enrichment program.

These types of programs I refer to as franchise programs. A franchise program attaches itself to an already successful and existing larger program. It can also be a packaged program from a larger company designed to create systemic change throughout a school district. Still, it can be a component of an overall existing program that works in conjunction with the overall vision of that existing mother program. Some examples of each one of these will serve to clarify this concept.

An enrichment program was established at my school to serve the accelerated students of a school with special activities. Every year the director of the program solicited ideas from the teaching staff on sessions that they would like to conduct. One such enrichment session involved the card game of bridge, yet another involved water bottle rocket construction and another was an entire class in cartooning. All of these are connected to the larger operating enrichment program umbrella. The school district financed the program and all of its components. There was a summer enrichment program involving both science and art. Instructors from all spheres served to create an interdisciplinary learning experience for two weeks in the summer for over 50 students. I worked as a volunteer assisting in dance and music programs and I acted as an instructor in mathematics, science and art. I operated a component program for the larger summer enrichment venue. Another program example occurred when my school district pursued a packaged program that was to connect students and revitalize student morale and achievement. Teachers went to workshops and helped develop an overall schoolwide concept. Some students were selected as leaders and an entire grade level of students as the participants. All three of these types of franchise programs addressed the funding issue prior to the existence of the new enrichment program. A franchise alleviates some of the stresses and burdens on a program director, yet it has its caveats. The freedom in creating and designing an overall vision and operating vision for these types of franchise programs are limited. There is already a set format that these programs follow. Understanding the limitations of an adjunct program and visions of the larger program are necessary. The final type of program is what I refer to as fully structured.

The fully structured program entails creating the visions for the program, gathering the funding for the program and enlisting the services of staff and selecting student participants. The fully structured program encompasses all aspects from its initial goal through its strategic development. This type of approach to an extracurricular enrichment program provides the largest positive transformative change opportunities of all of the types of program structures. Both of my mentors in this field put in the hours, weeks, months and years necessary to create enrichment programs that have stood the test of time and provided transformative experiences for many individuals. Whether the program is initiated by an individual or a group of individuals, it will take a concentrated effort on all aspects of program building to accomplish the goal. By looking at the other three types of programs, and more especially experiencing a fully structured program, will provide the knowledge necessary to create a fully structured enrichment program.

Before I created what was to be my final extracurricular enrichment program, I had first been introduced to a fully structured program as a summer college credit course for teachers. We were immersed in constructivist and experiential learning approaches. All that participated understood the vision of the weeklong program and the products and goals we were to produce during the program. I went on to participate in at least half a dozen of these college-sponsored programs. Through these programs, I was led to my involvement in another long-existing fully structured program. I participated on multiple levels in these programs, becoming fully immersed within it, I gained an understanding of its operations, mechanics and structures. Fully structured programs are the most demanding and equally the most satisfying.

With the knowledge of all four program structures, individuals or groups should have the basis for developing their own extracurricular enrichment programs. Looking at as many aspects as I can recall from my experiences and imparting that knowledge to others will hopefully promote transformative and enriching developments in our most important resource, our offspring. Not everything worked perfectly. Oftentimes, I would have to make adjustments because unforeseen issues cropped up. Still, by following through and maintaining the integrity of the original overall vision, the programs managed to succeed. If it is the first time developing an extracurricular enrichment program, controlling the size of the program will be important. It's like the old adage of you can't eat the chicken whole. I recommend a small afterschool program that lasts a specific amount of time. Developing all the components of an enrichment program will be more manageable if the time is limited and the goal familiar to the program director or leader. An individual classroom teacher, which is what I am or was, can create all four of the program types and have them be successful. With each program I worked with, my knowledge increased as did my motivation to make things better. Though at times I felt exhausted, frustrated and maybe a bit disillusioned, I met the challenges of each session, and in the end, was rewarded with transformative enriching success for the participants and myself. An emphasis on various transformative experiences allows for individuals to grow and develop above their original capacity. That may be, by definition, enrichment.

Keeping in mind some of the best practices in education such as differentiated learning, multiple intelligences, experiential learning, lateral thinking and higher-order thinking skills, enrichment programs can be built. The emphasis placed on skills acquisition can often be a driving force in all aspects of program development and continuation. Reflection on events during a single session and the overall performance of the program is crucial for a program director's growth. With reflections after each session, adjustments are more easily made that elevate the program.

The demands of social interaction for a prospective program director may be hard at first. Actually, they are hard all the time. Fundraising events become a part of a program director's lifestyle. Membership in community service groups is usually beneficial. Helping children is a mainstay of many nonprofit agencies. By interaction with members of the agencies, a network of allies and perhaps stakeholders can be created. A program director often needs to embody the vision of the program and might be the key morale officer for all the participants. Maintaining a positive attitude with an eye on the future are two things that work well for me. Not being afraid to fail or take risks are important attributes anyone wanting to create these types of programs should have. Follow the rules of the organization you belong to, and never forget the chain of command, as well as the important functions to maintain order and purpose.

I spent my entire career in one school district. I maintained cordial working relationships throughout my tenure. Much of my success was due to support from principals, curriculum directors and superintendents. Never forget that we succeed when others want us to succeed and help us to succeed. I'm grateful for my experience with my mentors and hope that anyone interested in developing these types of programs has someone they look up to in the education field. I've made a number of missteps while developing these programs but none of them severe enough to jeopardize the programs. It is a rewarding undertaking to develop an extracurricular enrichment program. It is demanding to initiate and maintain it, but it provides satisfaction for an educator that is very seldom replicated in the classroom. The experiences I gained throughout my career from these programs help develop all aspects of my life and teaching. Hopefully, you will find this book helpful and maybe a little inspiring or motivating.

1

Establishing a Vision (or I See What You're Saying)

Every school district has a vision statement and a mission statement. Most successful businesses also have vision and mission statements. An enrichment program must have a vision statement that is clear concise and concrete. Often, vision statements are abstract and far-reaching. For example, model car building can be used to demonstrate the differences in a vision statement for a large organization or school district and the vision statement for an enrichment program. Assuming there's interest in a model car building after school enrichment program, a common vision statement might be, "to instill the joy of building model cars." This type of vision statement will leave most facilitators and participants and other stakeholders confused by the ambiguousness of the word, "joy." Vision statements for enrichment programs should be much clearer and present more of what the facilitators want to see occur as a final goal or product.

A vision statement for a model car building club might be something like this, "Participants will build and paint model cars and participate in a culminating auto show presented in the school cafeteria with refreshments and displays." With this type of vision, you can explain what you plan to do clearly to the participants, the other stakeholders, school administrators, other facilitators, volunteers and the general public. You can see

DOI: 10.4324/9781003254911-2

that the program is heading toward a final display and presentation. This type of vision statement is more like a roadmap of the journey toward the success of your program. Concrete goals and products add a tangibility to an idea that can bring it quickly to reality. The creation of an enrichment program may require two types of visions. The first is the overall goal and product vision. What do you hope to accomplish by having this program; what can be expected at the end of the program? The more clearly defined the goal and product, the more acceptable the program will be to administrators and other stakeholders. Having a clear understanding of where you want to go will also make fundraising easier. The second type of vision statement involves the daily operation of the enrichment program. This vision of how each session will work is much like a lesson plan. It is made with broader strokes. The details get filled in as the session progresses. The first type of vision statement is used for presentation purposes to all stakeholders and to maintain the direction the program should be going. The second type of vision is to understand how each session will operate and provide a general format for all participants to develop a routine.

Your first vision statement will be used to gather allies and convince the administration and donors of the value of your program. If you go to a donor and present an abstract vision statement, they may not be willing to invest in it because of the unclear nature of what exactly you want to accomplish, such as instilling the joy of model car building. The single word joy is wide open to questioning, "what does that mean?" Remember, you're most likely trying to get money from somebody or trying to get permission to use facilities. Most individuals in a position to help the program have to answer questions presented to them by a higher authority. You, as the visionary of this program, must make it clear what is to be accomplished and how it is to be accomplished. The two types of vision statements needed for a successful enrichment program would be the long-term goal and product and the daily routine used to achieve the goal and product.

A facilitator or director must have a clear picture in their mind of what each day is going to entail much like a lesson plan utilized in class. From the moment the participants arrive at the program site to the moment they leave requires a clear plan of action. Program leaders need to have all the details in mind if they are to be successful with their program. By knowing how each day of the program will operate, the leaders can determine if the daily procedures lead to the final goal and product. Though there are various different ways enrichment programs come into being, the director of the program must see the complete picture in order for it to be successful.

Whether the program developed spontaneously and organically or whether it was thoroughly planned out, each type of program is going to require that the director and leaders see the same vision and work to accomplish that vision. Open communication between participants, facilitators, staff and other stakeholders will not only create a much richer and more successful program but will help keep the program on track when it inevitably goes astray. The question is how do you develop a workable vision for the program?

One of the first questions program directors should ask themselves is, what type of lens will we be viewing this program under? By lens, I mean the perspective, the overall driving idea or concept. Strong concepts such as skill development and application of knowledge should be at the forefront of these lenses. Take, for example, skill development, the leaders can ask themselves what type of skills are we teaching? Is it model building or is it direction following, step-by-step procedures, intricate hand–eye coordination and the application of mathematical scale? What the leader has to do is break down what is going to happen into the component parts that make it happen.

Another example might be mural painting. A local amusement park had a large fenced-in area that was devoid of color or images. I was asked to put together a team of students and their parents to paint a large mural on the fence. To do this, participants had to gather resources, many of which were donated, take a drawing transferred onto a larger scale and paint the image. The overall skills that the participants acquired ranged from speaking to local hardware store owners and paint store owners to gather the resources to taking a design on paper and transferring it to the actual fence, then mixing the paint and following the pattern to complete the large-scale work by the deadline. This presents the large-scale view of the program or the culminating project.

With the large-scale vision created, the program now needs the session-by-session vision to be developed. There are a number of reasons that you want to have this vision of what each day of your program should look like and what should occur during the time. Just as the large-scale vision of the culminating project in the overall skills that will be taught is important in fundraising and getting buy-in from stakeholders, the daily operations of your program will also be important in convincing stakeholders to buy into the program. That is not the only reason participants need a clear understanding of what is expected. Each day, the staff need a clear understanding of what is to be accomplished and, of course, the director has to have that clear vision. Much like lesson plans, the director program, coordinator or leader needs to know what everyone should be doing during the time the program is in operation. In the mural painting program presented earlier, the first thing students and parents did each day on arrival was to take attendance. This is a priority in a classroom and should happen in an extracurricular activity. It is a management detail that cannot be overlooked and is absolutely necessary for fundraising, the justification of the existence of the program, the continuation of the program and for insurance liability. Attendance must be taken. This program started in the morning and ran the entire day. Meals and breaks needed to be provided and scheduled. Supplies needed to be delegated. Work needed to be supervised and cleanup needed to occur. There was a general layout of what was to happen every day. If someone was to ask me as the director what I plan to do every day, I would start with attendance, meal or snack, gathering of supplies, assigning duties, scheduling breaks and lunch and finally supervising cleanup and supply management. With that type of clear vision, a program director can talk very accurately to all stakeholders and explain what they should see when they arrive at the site of the program.

Using a ship analogy, the overall vision of the program would be like the goal of getting to an island. The operational vision will be how the boat's crew manages the boat in order to get to the island. So here we have an overall vision and an operational vision and that's how we can refer to them in the future. When acquiring funds and permissions, you present the overall vision, and for clarity, you talk about the operational vision. The clearer these two visions are in the minds of the leaders of the program, the more successful the program will be.

Determine what the final goal is and/or the final project. This is the very beginning of your extracurricular enrichment programs vision. Once you know what you're trying to achieve, you can break down the skills needed to achieve that goal or product. Next, you want to list the skills that all the participants will acquire or require for the project to be successful. Using model car building as an example, you could say building a model car was the skill. That is not a very accurate or convincing explanation of the skills. To build a model car, you need fine motor skills, so that would be one of the skills taught. Eye–hand coordination is another very important skill needed and enriched. Product assembly is an important skill used by manufacturing worldwide. Following directions and looking at a schematic to produce a scale version of a real-life machine is a transferable skill on both a small scale and a large scale. Presentation of a product and competition are other skills that can be incorporated in this overall vision of the model-building program. A facilitator or creator of a program has got to look at the more basic functions of what is happening to define what skills are going to be taught and acquired. With an overall vision, the program director should be able to explain the goals and the skills necessary to achieve a functioning and successful program.

Moving on to the operational goals, the program will need a step-by-step procedure for every session of the program. These procedures should be consistent and practiced throughout the entire length of the program. If the first thing that participants do is sign in for attendance and get a snack, that is what should happen every single day the program is in operation. This part of the project is similar to lesson plans.

Utilizing the model-building program, we can create an example of an operational vision.

- ◆ Participants will sign in for attendance and pick up a snack and eat together in the workroom.
- ◆ Participants will go to the storage area and select their project and return to the work area.
- ◆ Supplies will be distributed to each participant.
- ◆ The instructor will circulate around getting each project started.
- ◆ During the main body of the program, participants will be building their models and instructors will be around to supervise and assist.
- ◆ At the end of the session, cleanup of the work area and storage of projects will be completed.
- ◆ Participants will be accounted for as they exit the program.

The operational vision of the program does not need to be finely detailed but more broadly presented. Each day will present different problems and challenges and adjustments will have to be made. Having an operational vision will keep all participants and staff focused on the final goal of the program and facilitate a much higher probability of success.

The two types of visions, overall vision and operational vision, give all involved a clear picture of what is expected and what is to be achieved. These two visions allow other stakeholders to clearly understand and buy into the program and its goals more readily. Without the establishment of these two types of vision, a more haphazard approach to the program will occur, lending itself to failure and unforeseen difficulties that could disrupt or terminate the program. There will always be challenges and unforeseen events but having these two visions at the forefront will allow the reestablishment of focus and a correction of the course of the program if necessary.

There are both similarities and differences in standard school-day classrooms and extracurricular enrichment programs. The classroom management skills of a teacher are necessary for any successful afterschool enrichment program. The motivation behind the types of participation in both standard school-day classrooms and enrichment programs is different. Understanding the most significant similarities as well as differences of these two programs is one more tool necessary for the success of these types of programs.

Just like in a regular classroom, the person in charge needs to know who is in attendance. Participation and accurate attendance are crucial for success in classrooms and in these types of extra-curricular programs. The importance of taking attendance for an extracurricular enrichment program cannot be over-stressed. Who is there and who is not is a vital statistic to determine the success of the program. At one of my summer weeklong pro-grams, we had 100% attendance. All the participants and stake-holders were amazed at such dedication of the students. It was that 100% attendance, verified by roll sheets and other documen-tation, that allowed for further fundraising. Accurate manage-ment is crucial to the success of these outside the school-day programs. Another similarity is in the recognition of a hierar-chy of authority. Eventually, the buck stops somewhere but along the way, it's quite a journey, and usually, the person in charge of these programs is at the bottom of the totem pole. Knowledge of the proper channels and chain of command will ensure a more positive response.

This brings us to one of the biggest differences between the two types of environments. The leadership of the extracurricular enrichment program is more like a director than any other type of administrator. Whether it is a solitary classroom teacher or an individual in charge of many teachers and students, the role of the director is the linchpin to the success of these programs. The director wears many hats and each one of these hats has to be worn with style. In other words, the director must do everything at peak levels of performance. Often, it's the director that moti-vates everyone. It's the director that gathers together all of the different participants. It's the director that is the facilitator and pilot of the program.

The director should be one of the original visionaries of the program. A director's buy into the program must be absolute. The dedication of the director is directly proportional to the ded-ication of all the participants. The director leads by example, they are not the sage on the stage but the most welcome ally through-out the program. The director sees to the needs of all members of the learning community. The director must handle situations that arise at a moment's notice with poise and focus. The role of the director is the single most important nonparticipant role in the program. Another difference between the extracurricular enrichment program and the standard school-day classroom is the motivation of the participants.

Whereas the participants in a standard school are most likely there for extrinsic motivation, if they are highly academic, it is the grade that is their motivation. If they are less inclined toward a positive view of education, they are there because of coercive measures. Either it is the reward of external payment in the form of grades, scholarships and acceptances to colleges and institutions or it is the fear of a punitive reprisal that motivates the participants. This is not so with an extracurricular enrichment program. The participants of outside the school-day programs are motivated by an interest and desire that comes from within themselves. This type of motivation is intrinsic motivation. The participants want to be there. The more inviting the program, the more the desire to be there. The more motivation to achieve, the more motivation to participate and that is why such lofty goals can be achieved with these types of programs.

Many classroom teachers and schools have high hopes and expectations of achievement for their students. Because schools are drawing on the entire student body, they can achieve these goals in high academics or in sports. Extracurricular enrichment programs can have the same lofty goals but on a smaller scale. It is a more individual-based level of extraordinary success. It is at this type of program level that students, staff and the director can find peak experiences of learning and growing because of the overall motivation to be there and the group's shared interest. Another similarity is the discipline and the maintaining of structure in both the classroom and the enrichment program.

A clear structure and well-defined expectations make a classroom successful. It will also make an enrichment program successful. Just as each child enters the classroom knowing what the discipline expectations are, every participant in the extracurricular program should be well aware of what the behavioral expectations will be. Unlike the classroom, where there is an overall school discipline structure, the extracurricular program is less formal and is apt to degenerate into a less disciplined structure relatively quickly. Keeping this in mind, the facilitators and director of the program must monitor the behavior of the students and make sure that they are on task and focused throughout the majority of the time in the program. Given too much leniency and less supervision can lead to even the most well-behaved students becoming discipline problems. It is not unheard of for some of the most talented and gifted students in the school to get themselves into situations that require administrative intervention. The staff and leaders of these extracurricular enrichment programs must be more aware of what their participants are doing than a normal classroom teacher. If some unforeseen event occurs it could bring about the termination of the program. Still, the facilitators, director and staff of the program must not be heavy-handed with discipline, so it can be a double-edged sword. They must maintain structure and discipline and still have a cooperative warm and inviting climate that facilitates growth and learning. Keeping in mind the differences and similarities in an extracurricular enrichment program and a standard school day will help provide a more successful environment for all the participants and stakeholders.

By examining the similarities and differences of these two types of learning environments, we see commonalities and important connections between the two. Though there are differences, and quite significant ones, those differences allow directors and facilitators of extracurricular enrichment programs opportunities to cut new ground in their education practices. The general underlying purpose of both the classroom and the enrichment program is higher-level learning skills. Every classroom teacher aspires to bring their students to the highest level, well the same is true with the director and staff of enrichment programs.

Throughout my career, I have found that these extracurricular enrichment programs can form in a variety of ways. There is a grassroots organic formation that can occur. There are also loosely structured programs that can be very successful. There are well-structured and well-planned out programs and there are franchise programs. An understanding of these types of programs allows administrators, teachers and other stakeholders a clearer understanding of the variety of ways extracurricular enrichment programs can come into being.

Throughout these various types of programs, the focus on the students' needs and learning opportunities will be apparent. I first got my understanding of an organic form of a program when I started working in a junior high setting and allowed a student to utilize a new piece of technology at that time, a computer. He would stay after school and work on designing various different classroom forms I utilized. It didn't take long for other students to notice that I was staying after school, and they also gravitated to my room. Before you knew it, I had a relatively large size youth hang out. This was not what I had originally foreseen. It was then that I realized that these young students were coming to my room because they had no other better place to go and I had resources such as paper, pencils, crayons markers, chalk and other interactive construction items available. Though many of the students came from very diverse and often underserved demographics, they all seem to cooperate and that sparked an idea. These young people needed something to do, something to create. Part of my early training was in art, and I had created a number of magazines and comic books. I knew how to create what would be called a mini comic book by taking ten 8 ½ × 11 sheets of paper and folding them hamburger style and stapling them at the crease. This made a mini comic book. I announced to the students that we would create a magazine. The idea was met with rousing enthusiasm. This magazine would allow the students to be creative and expressive and have something tangible to show for their work. And that is how the impossible dream machine program was started.

That was one example of an organically formed program. The students came, the director recognized their talents and the goal was established. Another type of semi-organic formed program can come about if a group of students with similar interests approach the administrator and ask for an opportunity to have some type of gathering with a specific purpose in mind, such as a game of role-playing strategy. A group of students in my school approached my principal and ask them if they could have a Dungeons and Dragons club. The principal knowing my interest in this particular game asked if I would act as a host in a kind of loose-fitting program to meet this group of students' needs. I took up the program and it grew from four students to nearly a dozen per session. Groups of students could have a number of interests from computer programming to model rocket building to robotics. Some of these programs would be initiated by the school administrator, who enlists a faculty member and gives them a rather loose mandate. With administrative support, there could even be some funding for the program. This type of program would be called loosely structured. It usually deals with a topic of interest of a select group of students. Because it has administrative support, the director will have more resources available than if the program was started by the teacher or staff member alone. Loosely structured programs have a vision and goals, but they are often created as the program is formed and the general-purpose and long-term goals may not be apparent. Sessions may not have a design but rather an impromptu organization. Now that we've examined organic and loosely structured programs, we should next look at a well-structured and designed program.

A structured program takes weeks if not months of preparation. A well-established overall vision and a well-defined operational vision are the very start of the program's structure. It is highly recommended that a handbook be developed that defines the full scope and sequence of the program. Whether this program is an afterschool semester, long single classroom or a series of instructors and multiple classrooms, the same format exists.

The last program I created was called the "The Ben Franklin School of Industry." It took three months to create all the material and gather the resources and establish collaborations with community leaders, school officials, donors, staff, volunteers and participants. The program was originally designed as a one-time, weeklong summer pilot project. This type of program structure often requires a grounding in educational theory. The creators of a well-structured program should base the overall vision on an established concept. I utilized constructivist educational theories and experiential learning as the basis for the program. Community connection and collegiate collaboration were brought about by the incorporation of the works of a local professor of economics. His report emphasized the need for skills in the local labor market. I utilized this report as a driving factor to create this program.

The work involved in creating a well-structured program is far more labor-intensive than any other program. The creators need to model this new program from already existing programs. By analyzing the structure of other successful summer programs, I was able to incorporate all the necessary forms and standards for operation. From start to finish, these types of programs need to be well-defined and have almost every contingency taken into account. The first time developing something like this might be best done at the classroom level. A program such as a week-long algebra math camp for 12 to 20 students might be a good place to start. To take on an entire multi-classroom independent operation might be too daunting to attempt by a single classroom teacher. Administrators familiar with the structure of complex programs might find this type of well-structured extracurricular enrichment program more manageable. It is recommended that a committee approach to at least gain an overall understanding of the demands and requirements to create a successful program should be utilized. As the visionary of this program, meeting with the participants, gaining knowledge of all of the necessary resources and listening to opposing points of view will help in the development of a successful program. This is a ground-up approach for building something brand new. Oftentimes, there are existing structures that a new program can fit into. I call this the franchise approach.

A franchise extracurricular enrichment program is based on something that already exists, whether it be a summer camp or an afterschool program designed to enrich students. It can also be a program designed by an outside source and demonstrated at a conference. If there is already an existing program that this new enrichment offering can connect to, the integration and transition will be much easier. In existing franchise programs, the groundwork in the original structure and the details have been ironed out and it is a well-managed operation. I was involved in several of these franchise programs. My experience participating as a volunteer and a staff member made it possible for me to create a well-structured program of my own. Before embarking on developing a well-structured program from the ground up, I personally recommend staff participate in these types of programs first. Even working as a summer camp counselor and observing how the summer camp operates will give new program creators a broader scope in which to view their idea and bring it to life. Schools may have an afterschool program already in operation. If an idea for a new extracurricular program fits into an existing structure, there is no need to reinvent the wheel. Take advantage of things that already exist and add to them. If the school district wishes to create something as broad as an afterschool enrichment program that encompasses multiple classrooms, then visitations to other districts that have such things already in existence are highly recommended. Observing what is already done and successful can only bolster the ability to create something new and substantial. Regardless of how the program comes into existence, its main emphasis must be on student enrichment.

We must never lose sight of the purpose behind what we are doing. The needs of students are not completely met during the school day. This is why these types of extracurricular enrichment programs are so vital to the educational experiences of the students. The constrictions of the school day and its mandated courses paint a broad stroke as to what students need from education. Extracurricular enrichment programs add the fine details necessary to provide each student with the optimum educational experience. A student's needs should be the main emphasis of why these programs come into existence. Identifying the needs is one of the first steps and this is where your overall vision comes into play. Sometimes, circumstances and global events may dictate a need for a program to build missing skills in students. The creation of the Ben Franklin School of Industry was brought about by communities' need for a skill-based workforce. Though the students did not know that certain skills were needed for employment in the local area, the facilitators and creators of the program were well aware of it. The designing and creation of these types of programs may be based on a student's desire to learn something new or the communities need for students to learn new skills. Either approach is viable for creating these programs. The creator must be aware of not only the students' but the community's needs. A broad understanding of the student body and the community in which they exist, and the resources available, will act as guidelines for the development of a successful extracurricular enrichment program. Grand visions of an elaborate program can act as a catalyst for a program's creation. I did not start with what I consider my opus program, the Ben Franklin School of Industry. It took years of experience to be able to execute that successful program. Just like the old parable of you can't eat the chicken all at once, visionaries and creators should start small and gain success and experience. Nothing can be more disappointing than putting a large amount of effort into something that doesn't materialize. Take advantage of existing structures and slowly gain the knowledge and ability to create more elaborate and complex programs.

2

The Impossible Dream Machine (or the Kids Lead the Way)

An examination of my first successful program and analyzing its various components and participants may prove valuable to the overall understanding of how an organic grassroots program forms. It was my third year teaching and I had a class full of reluctant students. These were seventh graders and many of them had not had much success in mathematics throughout their prior elementary school experience. Their behaviors may have limited their learning and their motivation toward school was most likely at a very low level. It is not uncommon for young teachers to get these types of classes. Throughout my career, I found classes of reluctant learners to be some of the most rewarding experiences in education that I have ever had. This particular class had a student that was very much influenced by the gang mentality that was sweeping the country at that time. The colors red and blue indicated the gang affiliation of their members. We were in a small town and therefore the gangs of the East and West Coast had not infiltrated the area, but their influences were felt. This particular young man was quite withdrawn and suffered from several different learning challenges. He spent most of the time in my class with his head down sleeping.

I wanted all of my students to have some interest in mathematics and I believed that mathematics is the one subject that

DOI: 10.4324/9781003254911-3

is neutral in its existence and accepting of all learners. Though the subject matter can sometimes be dry, the presentation does not have to be. I tried many different techniques to reach this young man. Finally, I happened upon the computer. At that time, computers were quite new, and I was able to get several in my classroom due to the efforts of a very astute and talented curriculum director. I introduced the young man to the computer, and he was fascinated by the technology. I used it as a reward for good class participation. If he tried in the class, he could stay after school and write his rhymes and raps on the computer and use the various fonts to design and embellish his work. He was so excited about the computer that he was in my classroom after school almost every day.

Several other students from that same class noticed that I was staying after school, and they started coming to my classroom. I had many different hands-on mathematical learning activities set up at various stations around my room as well as art material available. Some students just came to draw with chalk on the board. Other students wanted to color the large poster-type drawings of cartoon characters I had created and used to decorate my room. Within a week, I noticed that I had at least half a dozen students staying after school for as long as I would stay in my classroom. Many of these students came from underrepresented demographics and economically challenged environments. I did not want to have a young persons' hang out in my room. I needed to find a purpose for these young people and a goal that could be set that would maintain their interest and motivation. I had been working in the publication field, most especially the comic book field, for a number of years. Though I never met with any great success, I did get a large number of experiences that I could transfer to my teaching. I observed my students and drew some conclusions.

All of them seem to be interested in art and writing or in some way to express themselves. I talked to each one of them and got an idea of what motivated their creativity. I gathered them together and asked if maybe we should make a magazine, our very own magazine. The idea was not hard to sell. The students all jumped at it and wanted to be involved in putting their own ideas down on paper and seeing them in print. Even my reluctant learner at the computer wanted some of his poems published. I had been familiar with a very inexpensive way of constructing a small magazine. Merely by using 8.5 x 11 sheets of paper and folding them hamburger style, a booklet can be made. With two staples along the spine, a semiprofessional publication can be created.

When I was hired by the district, one of the stipulations of my hiring was that I would become the yearbook advisor for the high school. For the first two years of my teaching experience, I held the yearbook advisor position. My familiarity with assigning duties and setting deadlines would come in handy for this soon-to-be fledgling program. By developing a deeper understanding of each student's needs, desires and goals, I was able to craft literary and artistic assignments that the students would be motivated to complete. On the first day of our enterprise, we mapped out how big our magazine was going to be, who was going to do what and when it was going to be finished. All the resources needed to complete these tasks I had to provide. We met three times a week: Tuesday, Wednesday and Thursday. Not all students could come every day, but they at least could come one time a week. The students would arrive directly after school and get right to work. They were very intent on what they were doing, their conversations were polite and an overall positive learning community was developing. Each student showed a general interest in the project and respect for all the participants. The demands both mentally and physically that I had placed upon myself were quite daunting.

After a full day of teaching, I had to continue for another hour to an hour and a half in an even more demanding environment. The ratio of students to instructor was six to one and each student required my attention during each session. I had to circulate around the room to check on each student's progress and oftentimes managed two to three tasks at the same time. Though exhausted at the end of the day, I did find it quite rewarding. The energy and enthusiasm of a young teacher must never be taken for granted. The older I get the less energy I have, but at that time, I seemed quite exuberant toward my creation. I did not have a vision other than I was making a magazine with a number of students. I had done this same project in art school. I had created a comic book magazine by taking a collaboration of work from various artists and writers and putting them into one anthology. This was going to mimic my past publication.

It didn't take long before other colleagues noticed the students in my classroom after school, along with their behavior and dedication. By word-of-mouth, the school administrators were made aware of the activities in my room after school. I was visited by the full administrative staff, and they observed the students. Many of the students were frequent flyers in their offices. These office visits were not due to good behavior but rather some difficulty between the students and other teachers. My administrators were extremely impressed. Students that they felt were not only underserved but presented educational challenges for themselves and other classmates were functioning at levels they had never witnessed. Motivation, creativity and a desire to express oneself can transform even the most reluctant learner into an educational powerhouse. My administrators wanted to play a role in this type of program's success. They willingly offered me resources and their ideas on how to improve the program. One of the key components of any afterschool program is food. The school administrators had the cafeteria prepare snacks for my students for the days that they stayed after school.

The availability of food and the enjoyment the students were getting out of the program attracted their friends to my room. It wasn't long before I had over a dozen students, ranging in abilities from gifted to challenged, working on a magazine. One commonality the students had was that they did not feel part of any school group. This afterschool program filled that void. That is how this program came into being. Students themselves with just a little bit of adult support pulled themselves together and created a learning community. Now, this is not to underplay my role in it, but to emphasize a student-driven grassroots organic program. As the program developed, we needed a name for our publication, what I was doing seem nearly impossible. It seemed like a dream but yet we were creating some type of publication machine. We called our program and publication "the Impossible

Dream Machine." The program produced two magazines and ran an entire year.

The interest in this type of activity was so strong that I created a two-week summer program on children's book writing. Though the Impossible Dream Machine was an organic grass-roots student-driven creation, the summer children's book program was more in line with a franchise program fitting into the summer school concept the district had already created. It was this first experience with creating an afterschool enrichment program that encouraged me to develop more programs. The sustainability of a program depends on a number of factors. Knowing when to bring the program to a close is an important part of the program's success. After four separate publications all stemming from the Impossible Dream Machine, I directed my energies to another even more enriching program. From my first experience, we should draw some of the important points that worked and look at the greater challenges the program faced.

Originally, there was no concept of the program. The program developed on the fly. That can be problematic because the creator of the program, the director, really does not have a sense of direction. That is what happened in the first few weeks that students arrived in my classroom. I had originally focused on only reaching one student when in fact I should have been focusing on reaching a larger body of students. The students are the most essential part of any program. One of the key things necessary to even have a program is students. My first program began itself as the students appeared. Not only did the original students come to the program, but they also brought their friends. There was no need for me to recruit or advertise this program. There was a void in a lot of these students' lives and this program offered an opportunity to fill that void. It is essential that we always consider what the student needs when building these programs.

The students will tell you what they need if you pay attention to them and get to know them. A knowledge of their background and interests is commonplace among teaching practices yet not employed enough. It is a slippery slope that every teacher must approach cautiously as they involve themselves with students outside of the school day. That is why it is very important to have an overall vision. I was lacking an overall vision when I first started. I was just providing a learning environment and safe supervision. The product, the magazine, is what drew everyone together. A common goal that is clear and obtainable yet lofty enough to instill pride in the participants is a catalyst for these types of programs. The idea that each student could see themselves in print and have their name and work recognized was extremely motivating. You know a program is working when it's time to go home and you have to usher out the participants. That is a very gratifying yet bittersweet reward for all the efforts the director and the staff put toward the students.

Knowing the talents and interests of the student, the director can then channel that talent in a direction that is beneficial to the overall program or learning community. In a broad sense, an extracurricular enrichment program is a functioning learning community. Students and teachers are both learning. For the fledgling director, the first program will be a more intense learning experience for them than the student participants. Deeper knowledge of the students in your program is very important. Taking attendance and keeping track of the whereabouts of each student is crucial to the program's success.

This concept became glaringly evident when the school administrators paid an impromptu visit to one of my afterschool sessions. They were thoroughly impressed with the focus and conduct of all the student participants. Their eyes were also on my desk and they certainly examined the roster and the hall pass roster. Though I was quite a new teacher my mentor had instilled in me the need for attendance and knowing where all the students are at all times. This bit of managerial skill aided in the overall appeal of the program to the administrators. They knew that their general overall operating rules for their building were being adhered to even after normal school hours. They were very pleased to see students often labeled as reluctant learners engaged in a task and interacting with other students in a positive manner. They also recognized that many of the students came from underserved demographics. All these factors played a role in the administrative support the program received. The program was given or rather the students were given the necessary paper art supplies and other materials to make the magazine publication possible. We were given permission to publish 100 magazines. Getting from the magazine vision to the actual magazine production is another part of creating a successful program.

The initial enthusiasm of the overall participants in the program was resoundingly positive. This enthusiasm would ebb and flow depending on the moods of the students. Sometimes, a student would be missing because of a suspension or other disciplinary action. Bringing these students back into the fold is no easy task. Getting a seventh, eighth and ninth grader to complete a project is a lot easier said than done. As the magazine developed, the work involved increased, and students that had not done that much work throughout their early educational careers were now putting forth significant effort. It is easy for these types of students to get distracted. Maintaining the proper level of enthusiasm and motivation is key. How a director accomplishes this varies with the overall goals of the program and the temperament of both the students and the director. Sometimes you get what you get.

With the Impossible Dream Machine, it meant that some students did not finish their story or their drawing and somehow it would have to be included in the book finished or not. The composition of the participants will dictate the overall performance of the program. The more accustomed the participant is to completing a project, the more successful the program participants will be. The dedication of the students to these types of extracurricular activities will control the overall quality of the goal or product of the program. This is true for all demographic groups from gifted students to reluctant learners. More than any other type of program formation, the grassroots organic approach seems to be the most student driven. A loosely planned program has a combination of student interest and the director's motivation.

I had been given an opportunity to teach a computer programming class in the computer lab at the junior high where I was teaching. The original class was to teach one of the more common programming languages. HTML programming language was just coming into being as the internet was growing. I had experience programming in HTML and approached the administration to say that I would teach HTML rather than one of the basic computer languages because it seemed timelier. When the students in the class found that with a few lines of code they could view their creation immediately online their enthusiasm for the programming language HTML grew. A group of friends took a greater interest in webpage creation. They were also interested in acquiring more powerful computers. I presented an idea for creating an online mathematics game. I had been working for a publisher that wanted a greater web presence. The initial four students embraced that idea wholeheartedly. Thus, the Absurd Math team was born. Initially, four students took part in an after-school program with the goal of creating an online mathematics game. There were a number of interesting ways to apply the programming language of HTML and JavaScript. It is to be noted that all the participants in this particular program also had accelerated academic careers. Many of them were classified as gifted and talented.

This composition of program participants led to the creation of one of the first visual mathematics games on the internet at that time, Absurd Math. The group of participants grew over the next few years to about a dozen. Eventually, the students were hired as freelance programmers by companies with whom I had already been contracted. This type of program, though loosely formed, had a more deliberate vision in mind. The concept of using the internet for learning was just being introduced. It seemed very natural that this group of students would want to create a learning application for the internet. Breaking down the program into its component parts will demonstrate how this loosely constructed program can work.

The first and most necessary component of the program was already there, a classroom full of students. From the classroom population, a group of friends with common interests emerged. The vision for the program needed to be created. As the director or future director of the program, I listened to the students discuss the various applications of the programming languages that create a webpage. The mathematical connection between algorithms and moving further in a game was discussed. The overall vision of the program was created by listening to the students and then forming it into a tangible goal. As the project progressed, we incorporated other team members and their programming and art skills. The operational vision was arrived at by group consensus. All participants and the director discussed what should be accomplished each day and who should accomplish each task. Duties were assigned and each session proved quite productive. There was joint empowerment in the creation of the program.

The overall supervision still fell on the shoulders of the director. Gentle guidance was utilized to move the discussion in a productive direction that all members could agree upon. Consensus on the overall product was important to the success of the program. An operational budget and administrative permissions were necessary to ensure the success of the program. The budget for the program was small because the resources were readily available. By informing the administration of my intention to conduct an afterschool computer programming enrichment activity, the program got the needed food supplements from the cafeteria. The component of food cannot be overstated. These are all growing humans, and they require nutrition. The nutrition offered at the beginning of the program may be the greatest enticement to participate in the program. Following the existing school structure, taking attendance and monitoring the whereabouts of all students still matter even when dealing with well-behaved, well-motivated and highly intelligent participants. It is not unheard of for some star students to foolishly climb out restroom windows onto school roofs in plain sight of the general public. To save your school and yourself from embarrassment, know where your students are at all times. To gain a deeper understanding of how the formation of grassroots organic programs occurs, we will need to look at the type of students attracted to both programs and look for commonalities.

Originally, there was no concept for the Impossible Dream Machine. It wasn't even on the horizon. My initial motivation was to try to reach a very reluctant student that had been impressed with the gang mentality. The student showed no interest in education and was only there because he was being forced. He was refusing to participate in any of the educational opportunities provided. His interest in the computer, which was a new technology at the time, is what encouraged me to utilize this technology to reach this reluctant student. He fitted into a number of categories of underserved students. Staying after school to work with a piece of technology that he may never have had an opportunity to use except in the school setting was enough motivation for him. The fact that I let him create what he wanted to create, and I didn't edit it increased his enthusiasm. Once, I had his interest in the computer I was able to utilize it to get him to have some interest in my class. Computer use after school was both an intrinsic and extrinsic reward for the student. Little did I know that his presence in the classroom would attract more students from similar underserved demographics.

The junior high where I was teaching was located in the center of town. The students that stayed after school to utilize my classroom all walked from their homes to the junior high school. The initial composition of half a dozen students all consisted of underserved demographics and lived within walking distance of the school. All of them had an interest in art, writing, poetry, comic books or had yet to discover any latent talents that they had. Each one of the students lacked major group affiliation. None of them were involved in athletics. None of them were involved in academics. None of them had ever stayed after school of their own volition. The only time many of them stayed after school was for punitive retaliation for their behaviors. All of them enjoyed a somewhat free classroom environment where there were no safety concerns and resources were available.

My classroom was filled with many learning stations, and through the budget, I purchased a number of hands-on mathematical learning tools. The students could construct robots or even scale model buildings from the materials in the classroom. Many of them were just interested in using paper and pencil and markers available to write down their thoughts. What surprised me, was that during the school day, many of the students did not associate with each other but coming to my room after school they all started to associate, cooperate and participate with each other. Some of them stayed after school because there was nothing to go home to or home was very stressful. In a quiet classroom away from the commotion of the normal school day, students that were under social stress could find peace and relaxation. This welcoming environment created by the artwork, my cordial personality and all of the learning resources available attracted the students and kept them coming back. It is to be noted that a local youth center had recently closed down and many of the students had spent their afternoons just hanging out at the youth center. They were now utilizing my room as their youth center.

I really didn't want to be a youth center counsel. That was not how I wanted to spend my afterschool hours. I did have a desire to create something and to work with people. My interest in magazine production artwork and writing played a major role in the creation of this program. My belief that every person has artistic and writing talent was not dampened by this program. More so, it was encouraged and promoted by the program. Once we had decided to produce a magazine, more students were attracted to the program. There were no advertisements announcements or any other promotion of the program other than the word-of-mouth of the students that were participating in the program. It is to be noted that once the administration became aware of the program and supported it, they began to steer other reluctant students in the program's direction. Whether it was by friendship with current members of the program or the administrator's gentle hand guiding a student toward the program, a variety of types of students filled my classroom and helped create the magazine.

Not only did we have reluctant students due to behavior and social conditioning, but we also had gifted and talented students that had not found their place in the school environment. This is not to say it was a group of outcasts; it was more like a group of people that did not find themselves until they had a common goal and purpose provided by the extracurricular enrichment program. Some students lived in the suburbs of the school district and their parents would drive them home after the school day had concluded. While other students walked home to the urban environment and often dealt with stressful home situations. The commonalities that occurred between these diverse student groups are what made the Impossible Dream Machine such a success.

Students that never associated with each other or talked with each other or even knew of each other's existence were now drawn together with a common goal in mind. Each one of them wanted to achieve this goal. Some had greater motivation than others, but the motivation to achieve something for themselves was there. The Impossible Dream Machine was a gathering of diverse student groups and individuals. The uniqueness of a magazine format that allowed for individual expression facilitated an ease of entry into the program even after it had started. Ideas and the works of individual students could be incorporated into the magazine because we had no set page limit. The size of the magazine was determined by the submissions from the students. As the director, I would fill in any gaps that the magazine had to make it more cohesive.

The team of students that created the program, which we will call Absurd Math, was not diverse. They all had common interests in computer programming and academic achievement. By comparing the two groups, we will hopefully see what type of bonds make for a cohesive program and learning community. The members of the programming team for Absurd Math had a motivation to achieve and accomplish something with the new technology. This was similar to the young man who I introduced to the computer in the magazine creation program. He, like the members of the Absurd Math team, was motivated by technology. The instant gratification of work that the internet provides also acted as a motivator for the members of the web game development program. Each member that worked to create the online game brought their own set of skills and contributed to the knowledge base of the overall program and learning community. Much the same as the Impossible Dream Machine magazine, the program grew and various new members brought their ideas and skills to the program.

The sharing of skills and the cooperation between members of each program is another important component to a successful overall program. When students teach other students, we as educators have reached a level that we aspire to from the very beginning of our educational career. The student that becomes the teacher of other students helps to strengthen the program and this develops within each student a sense of self-worth and belonging. Though both groups had a lot of personal differences, the commonality of trying to belong to something worthwhile and working with others was a key factor in the success of both programs. The students' need for stronger affiliations with other students became apparent in a cohesive welcoming and friendly program atmosphere. If a student feels like an outsider, no matter how motivated they are and how enticing the program is, they will be reluctant to participate fully or even slightly.

As a director of a program, making sure that each participant feels welcome and as part of a larger group cannot be stressed enough. Each one of these programs had several very friendly and outgoing individuals. As a director, I utilized their extroverted nature to help create that friendly welcoming atmosphere that brought more students to the program and kept those students that were there coming back. The atmosphere of your program will be created by the director, the students and the project itself. Multiple entry points need to be considered. Each student that comes to the program needs to find their place in the program. It becomes the director's task to assist the student in finding their place and becoming part of the learning community and program.

Some key components that we should take away from these two types of extracurricular enrichment programs are student interest and motivation, a challenging yet obtainable goal or project and ease of entry into the program. Not all programs can be entered after they begin. Those that can have a higher probability of success than those that start with a more rigid structure. The fluid form of a program that allows for individual differences but maintains the integrity of the program will find greater success than a program with strict limitations and a need for student conformity. This is not to say that those types of programs are not important and will not be successful; it's just saying that an organic grassroots program and a loosely structured program do not fit into that category. The organic program will grow itself and it is the director's job to manage and guide it. A loosely structured program will have a framework that is well defined, but the overall operation of the program may change as it progresses. We must keep in mind students' needs, overall school policies and operations and classroom management in order to prevent the program from going in the wrong direction or stopping before the final project. Both the organic and the loosely structured program can fail if the director and the students lose motivation and the goal becomes clouded and unclear. The overall vision of a program needs to be a constant factor in maintaining the program's direction and purpose.

3

Semi-Structured Programs (or I'll Do the Heavy Lifting and You Pay the Bill)

A semi-structured concept is where the program adheres to the overall operational principles of the school or organization that is supporting the program yet does not conform to the standard program structure of other established club and team organizations. Rigidly structured programs such as sports teams, civic clubs and other pre-existing student organizations, all have a set format with elected officers, official budgets, bank accounts and sets of rules and regulations. A semi-structured enrichment program may not even have an operating budget; it certainly would not have a bank account and general rules and organizational structure would not have been created at that time. The loose format allows the director and students the freedom to develop the program to meet their needs and still function within the parameters of the organization that is housing it. Standardly structured groups and organizations have bylaws that govern their operations. A semi-structured extracurricular enrichment program will not have these bylaws. It will have a fluid structure that allows for the development of the program and its goals. The loose structure allows the formation of a more natural enrichment

DOI: 10.4324/9781003254911-4

program while still containing some of the major components of all other organizations.

Throughout my experience, the semi-structured concept has proven to be one of the most effective ways to start a program. Most often, a burgeoning program starts with some sort of spark, an idea that comes from an administrator, a teacher or the students. Throwing a rigid structure immediately at this program is almost a sure way to prevent it from coming into existence. The creative process and the enthusiasm generated by something new and unique will be dampened when it is forced to conform prematurely to the overall structures of existing clubs and programs. Most school districts have strict bylaws as to how these clubs and organizations can be formed. When an extracurricular enrichment activity is brought into being, it will not have any of these structures present at its onset. All participants are going to need to examine what type of structure they can work within and still maintain the integrity of their original concepts and ideas. This is a creative process and adherence to a more rigid structure will almost certainly slow the process if not stop it from occurring. Keep in mind that the school or organization has general operating principles already in existence and that these principles must be followed whether it is an afterschool mentorship or participation in a schoolwide project. If the director or adult in charge recognizes and embraces the operating principles of the organization that is sponsoring or will be sponsoring the program, a more fluid and successful start is likely.

Because a semi-structured program lacks the number of checks and balances that organizations have placed to prevent the exploitation of funds or individuals, the leaders of these programs must be cautious and judicious about how they go about initiating this overall activity. Giving participants free rein and little guidance will most likely result in the program's failure. The creative process of bringing an afterschool enrichment program into being is delicate and sometimes temperamental. Participants and the director will have predisposed ideas of what the program should look like and not all members will agree throughout the process. Sometimes, the director will have to play the role of the authority and establish set rules guidelines and operating principles to keep the program moving forward. It will be noted that usually these types of programs have support from a more established administration. Directors that choose to bring a program into being without informing their immediate superiors of the program, its guidelines and purpose are going to meet with resistance if not find that the program will be immediately shut down. Directors must understand they are operating within an established sphere of rules and regulations. They may not be aware of the subtleties that a school district or other organization must utilize to maintain functionality.

Throughout my tenure as a teacher, I blundered a number of times. It might be beneficial to expose my failings so that others do not repeat my same mistakes. When I initially started my teaching career, I was the yearbook advisor. The job of teaching for the first time and advising the yearbook proved quite challenging and the stress caused me to make some critical mistakes. One mistake occurred when in order to advertise the yearbook I instructed my students to place sticky notes on every locker throughout the school advertising the yearbook. Every locker had bright yellow, orange, green or white sticky notes with printed messages about buying a yearbook. The publisher had provided these sticky notes and suggested placing them on student lockers. I followed the publisher's suggestion and upon arriving at school the next morning, I was immediately directed to the principal's office. It seems I had neglected to ask permission to do such a thing and had created a mess for the building's maintenance department. Sitting in the middle of the principal's office was a huge garbage bag filled with all the sticky notes, a frowning principal and an extremely unhappy building superintendent. I was instructed in no uncertain terms to not ever do this again, that I caused undue chaos at the start of the school day. Had I asked permission, I would've found out that the sticky notes may have been effective to alert the students to the yearbook but they would be extremely difficult for the janitors to pick up as they stuck to the floor. Red-faced, ashamed and thoroughly disciplined, I went back to the drawing board to try to figure out how to inform students of the yearbook sales.

Another foolish violation of school policy occurred when I was working as a coach for a sports team. It seemed that in order to participate in a specific athletic event, students needed to leave school early. The head coach and I asked permission for the team to leave earlier than normal to prepare for this event. Permission to leave was denied. My head coach decided to take it upon himself and instructed all the athletes to have notes written by their parents excusing them early from school that day. This deceptive practice led to another trip to the principal's office for the head coach and me. What appeared to be a workaround of school rules, was in fact a negative life lesson given to our athletes. The understanding of the school's principal was much appreciated. He reprimanded us and told us that we just taught some of the best students in the school to lie to authority. Both the head coach and I were stunned at the blatant negative behavior that we had instructed our athletes to do. Not only had we involved the athletes in the lie but it also involved their parents. The fact that we didn't get harsher disciplinary action against us was attributed to the understanding and kind nature of the school's principal. I am not sure that I would not have been far more indignant about the overall event. It was a good beacon for future decisions and behaviors that I would be involved with as I continued my teaching career. Never ever introduce your students and participants to negative behavior to get around rules. Rules are established for a certain reason. You may not agree with that reason but until the rule is changed you must conform to the rule.

Even when I was the president of an organization with the maximum amount of power, I still needed to be cognizant of bylaws, rules and regulations. Violating established rules, most especially by a leader, sends a very bad message of, "Do as I say not as I do." Both of these examples occurred with already established organizations within the school. Because of these two crucial experiences, I was able to apply the knowledge of my mistakes and prevent them as I created my extracurricular enrichment programs. The old adage, "it is better to be told to stop than told no," is not something to be followed within an organization. If a group of students and/or director have an idea for an afterschool program, it needs to be presented to the immediate supervisor. If you fear the supervisor will say no, then the program is most likely not going to occur. It will become the job of the director and the students to convince the supervisor of the importance of this program and how all contingencies have been addressed to ease the stress and concern of that supervisor. Remember, most supervisors have someone that they answer to, not just the school superintendent but the general public and school board. The director and students are the proverbial low people on the totem pole. With all of the caveats in mind, the creation of a semi-structured extracurricular enrichment program can take place and be successful.

One of my most successful semi-structured extracurricular enrichment programs took place the summer of my fifth year of teaching. I was teaching seventh grade and one of my classes was an accelerated pre-algebra course. The students and I had developed a good rapport and they were sad to see the summer break coming, in one sense because it meant the end of their math course and time with me. Neither the students nor I wanted our experience in mathematics and the enjoyment of each other's company to end. I proposed to the students to have a one-week summer class that introduced algebraic concepts that they would be encountering in their algebra one course in their eighth-grade year. The idea met with a great reception. The problem came in picking the dates for the one-week session. Not all the students that wanted to participate could make it in the same week. Various other different obligations precluded their participation at that time. We decided to offer the program at two different times. The program would be called Summer Algebra Camp. Not too original but it was clear about its purpose.

Two components necessary to have an extracurricular enrichment program were in place. There was a director and there were participants. The rest was still to be decided. Where does a young energetic enthusiastic teacher with big ideas turn for help to make a program concept a reality? Where the program is to be held will dictate what parties need to be contacted and what approvals need to be acquired. Since schools are generally empty in the summer, my classroom would hopefully serve as the center for this program. Knowing where I was going to hold the program guided me to who I was to ask about having a program. It is very important to have a cordial and working relationship with the school administration or the administration of any organization. Without their help, their guidance and their knowledge, ideas and best intentions are not going to manifest appropriately. I went to my school's principal and proposed the one-week math camp to be held in two separate sessions.

My principal was overjoyed to find that there were students that actually wanted to learn math in the summer. He jumped at my offer to spearhead this program. I was given the room and access to resources readily available to classroom teachers during the normal school year. Resources such as copy paper, copy machines, overhead projectors or whatever was needed and generally used in the classroom. My principal was far more aware of the school's budget and general operations of the district. He put me in contact with the curriculum director. It should be noted, the curriculum director was a former principal of my school and I had a very good relationship with him as a principal and as the curriculum director. The arrangements for the tuition and my stipend were all done through the curriculum office and the business office of the school district so the process was seamless and I didn't have to do any of the financial planning myself. The curriculum director stated that the program had to be self-funded and my salary would have to come from the tuition paid for the program. There was a total of about 20 participants in both sessions of the program. The tuition was able to cover my salary and provide scholarships for any student that could not afford to pay for the session. This is one of the reasons that I call this a semi-structured program. The financial particulars did not have to be addressed by the director or anyone connected to the program. Outside experts handled all of the financing. It fitted into a standard procedure for finding extracurricular activities. Had I been responsible for gathering the tuition and paying for whatever was needed, as well as my salary, it would've been a fully structured program.

The overall vision of the program was created by the students and me. We decided to address some of the important math topics they would face in algebra one in the coming school year.

The operational vision was still missing. This is another part of a semi-structured program. Creating the operational vision after the program has been initiated is not something a fully structured program could possibly do. Recall, the operational vision answers particular questions that other stakeholders have about the program. I had met with such a warm reception from my principal and curriculum director that I did not need to have an operational vision prepared for them. If the program was to be successful, I would need to develop a thorough operational vision. The length of time a single session of a program runs greatly influences the details of an operational vision. If the program is only half an hour long for one morning a month, the number of activities needed will not be as extensive as a year-long weekly two-hour program. The math camp was to run for three hours each day for five days, which is very similar to a block schedule in a school day, unlike a standard math class with lecture notes followed by homework. (This is not to offend math teachers. It is just a standard template filled in with the teacher's own personal touches.) If students were going to come to learn math in the summer, they were going to want an exciting experience. My presentation of mathematics was always dramatic and entertaining in the early years of my teaching. Filled with energy and enthusiasm, I was jumping on tables wearing masks putting on costumes and imitating some of the more famous math teachers around the country that did similar dramatic presentations.

My operational vision for this type of program emphasized intellectual challenge and imaginative mathematical situations. I thought of the program more like a TV show than a class. Because I had no set curriculum and was not answering to any standardized test, I could stretch the envelope and present mathematics in an entirely different light. Another component of a semi-structured program is changing and adjusting plans as situations arise. The first week of the program had its rough spot areas where I was dissatisfied with my performance and presentation and the skill level of the challenges. I was able to address these either on a nightly basis or for the next week's session. Semi-structured programs allow for more change than a fully structured program with a much more set format. A semi-structured format allows the director and participants more freedom to go in directions that they are taken by their ideas and the situation. Be warned, this can lead to some difficulties and challenges.

Time management is one of the weak points of a semi-structured program. Because the operational vision is vaguer, the time involved to do an activity may prove problematic. Sometimes, an activity can be almost over before it starts. If the activity doesn't seamlessly fit into the program, the transition from one activity to another can be difficult and disjointed. At the end of one activity, there needs to be a smooth transition to the next activity. Semi-structured programs often don't take that into account. What can happen is an activity ends and a break is taken. Drawing the participants back into a new activity can take longer than expected and be more difficult than one would like. Then once everyone is back on the same page, the next activity starts slower and requires unfamiliar skills, and the reluctance of some of the participants might be noticed. If one or two participants lose interest in whatever activity is going on, more participants may follow suit. The new extracurricular enrichment program is going to have rough spots that may need to be ironed out in order to get the program to function successfully.

These rough spots will not have a contingency plan to address them and the director and staff must handle the situation quickly and efficiently. This will be very stressful and can sometimes bring out the worst in a director. The pressure to perform can take even the most even-tempered person and turn them into a tyrant. Once the director loses their perspective, it is very difficult to get it back that same day. It is recommended that there be more activities than there is time for the activities. When an activity ends abruptly, doesn't start correctly or finishes way ahead of schedule, a filler activity must be put into place. Semi-structured programs often do not have these contingencies addressed and the director and staff are left to create at a spur of the moment. Activities that run too long can interfere with other staff members' plans and programs. Even if there is only a director, an activity that takes too long can throw the entire program schedule off and makes it difficult to put it back on track. Being aware that time management is going to be an issue helps the creators of semi-structured programs anticipate these situations. Issues can arise in any type of program. Organic grassroots forming programs and semi-structured programs may have, potentially, more issues than a fully structured program. How each issue is handled will directly impact the overall effectiveness and success of the program.

During the last part of my teaching career, I hosted a semi-structured enrichment program after school every Thursday for three years. The program served between eight and 12 students ranging from ninth grade to 12th grade. The program came about when some of the students approached the principal and wanted to have a Dungeon and Dragons club. My principal was aware of my interest in what are known as role-playing games (RPGs). I knew a number of the students and was also aware that the majority of them fitted into the special needs category. I did have prior experience both good and bad with hosting Dungeons and Dragons games at a school.

Dungeons and Dragons once carried quite a stigma to it and was at the center of controversy. Currently, I do not believe that it carries the same stigma and concerns. Still, I was hesitant to call anything Dungeons and Dragons. I met with the principal and we discussed the format for an afterschool enrichment program. Although it was a game, it involved a number of special needs students and it acted as a socializing program. I incorporated problem-solving and nonviolent resolution of issues as a major emphasis of the games. The principal and I decided that we would call this program, "strategies and solutions in role-playing games." The afterschool environment, the entertaining elements of the game and the availability of refreshments made the overall atmosphere very inviting and cordial. The fact that nonviolent solutions to situations was the emphasis provided a creative venue for these ingenious problem solvers. The excitement over the game brought more and more participants to the program. This is one of the other concerns that a semi-structured program brings with it. With a structured program, the number of participants is already planned for and the space necessary for these participants is ensured. A semi-structured program may not have a participation limit placed at the beginning of the program. If a program population gets too big, it can lead to difficulties.

The capacity for participation in the program was a dozen students. Initially, there were six participants. Within two weeks' time, it had grown to eight participants with each student asking if they could bring a friend. Determining who could participate created some complexities I had not anticipated. Excluding students from a program is always a difficult choice. The resolution to this problem came through an overall consensus of the director and the participants. We determined together how many people could take part in the program and ensured that everyone had adequate time to play and enjoy the game. We decided on a first-come-first-served basis so no one was excluded from participating because they had to be selected. We decided that 12 was the maximum; there were eight participants at this time. The remaining four spots were filled in order of requests. Though some felt bad that they did not get to play everyone understood the first-come-first-served basis of selection. Having too many participants is a problem many extracurricular enrichment programs would like to have.

It will be advantageous for the creators and directors of semi-structured programs to know ahead of time the participation capacity of the program. This will not change the semi-structured fluid existence of the program. It will provide some needed grounding that will prevent overpopulation of the program to occur. Programs that are running smoothly can and will degenerate into chaos if they become overpopulated. What starts as fun and enthusiasm with the participants can quickly turn into dissatisfaction and create other interpersonal issues. As a general rule, I prefer a five or six to one ratio of students to adults. The maximum capacity for one adult to supervise and provide adequate attention is 12 students. This is not to say that 20 students can't be well served in a program by one adult facilitator. However, it is a concern that I have experienced myself while operating a fully structured program.

When a program becomes overpopulated, participants can potentially feel neglected and it is often the most self-reliant and positive members of the group. Because of their good conduct and amenable nature, these students often find themselves on the outside of the situation where they were once the center of attention. An adult supervisor tends to concentrate on the problems and not continue to support the positive nature of participants. It is not uncommon for one of the more effective members of the group to confront the director at the end of the session to let them know their dissatisfaction with the lack of attention they had been receiving. The old adage that the squeaky wheel gets the oil is often true. It does carry with it the neglect of the well-operating wheels. Being aware that overpopulation limits, time and level of involvement from adult facilitators will help prevent the neglect of participants.

Overpopulation can occur at any time in a program. One student may bring a friend without asking permission. Because the program is semi-structured and does not have a population limit placed at the very beginning, the situation where a student brings a friend can be quite awkward. Directors have an emphasis on cordiality so turning someone away may be physically impossible due to the location and timing and also the emotional difficulty. The best suggestion I can give to a director and staff is for them to increase their energy level and devote adequate attention to all members including the uninvited guest. How uninvited guests are treated will reflect directly on how participants feel that they are being treated. Extracurricular enrichment programs by nature need to be inviting and positive. It is easy to be inviting and positive when all things are running according to plan. It is when things are not planned for that challenges the director and staff to continue to be cordial, inviting and positive. When an adverse situation arises within the parameters of the program, the solution to the situation often dictates the success and overall longevity of the program.

During one of the sessions of the strategy role-playing game program, one participant let their behavioral issues manifest in the program and violence between two participants occurred. Because of the semi-structured nature of the program, immediate conflict resolution could be utilized rather than procedural consequences as dictated by the school. As the director, I had to determine whether this moment of violence merited ending the entire program, sending the perpetrator to the administration for further discipline or resolving it satisfactorily to all parties and continuing with the program. At this particular time, I stepped outside of school policy but maintained a structure that was consistent with other school policies. Both parties were privately admonished and an amenable solution between the two combatants occurred. Documentation of the incident took place and the parents of both students were contacted immediately. The quick response and the conflict resolution process were appreciated by both parents and an understanding of the behavioral challenges that both the students had was acknowledged. The school administration was informed of the situation and its resolution. My principal was appreciative of my quick response and solution. It is absolutely essential that when issues arise in a semi-structured or even a fully structured program that they are addressed with best practices at all times. Some situations have no best practice format to follow and a director or staff must use their discretion to find a sufficient resolution to the issue.

One such issue arose during my early years of teaching and facilitating extracurricular enrichment programs. A group of students and I had asked permission to utilize a room for a Dungeons and Dragons game. After the game, several of the students threw eggs at the house of a teacher that they had been having difficulty with throughout the year. The next morning, I was confronted by the teacher and accused of inciting the students by playing the game. The issue was brought before the principal and again the game we were playing was at the center of the problem. The stigma attached to the Dungeons and Dragons genre was hard to combat. It looked as though the game would have to come to an end due to the suspected behavior of some of the participants in the program. The teacher lacked any hard evidence to identify the students but was certain that they were members of the program. He neglected to inform the principal that there had been a year-long battle between students and himself. The principal was unwilling to attribute the action to the game without direct evidence of its connection. I took it upon myself to investigate and find the answer necessary to put things right with the teacher, the students, the principal and the game.

The rapport I had developed with those students in my class, as well as those that played the game, allowed me to convince the perpetrators to clean the house they had thrown eggs at during the night. The program was allowed to continue but I strongly admonished all participants to be aware of their behavior after each and every gaming session. Events beyond the control of a director or staff can often impact the overall health of the program.

Events outside of the program that impact the program are far beyond the control of its creators. There is very little chance to plan for many of these incidents. Still, when they occur positive, decisive and quick action must be taken. Letting a situation resolve itself may go in a direction that is adverse to the success of the program. These incidents are often rare and may not occur during the entire life of the program. If they do, how they are resolved will impact the overall success of the program. If an incident arises, don't bear the burden of its solution by yourself. Discussing with the school's leadership and your peers may provide some insight into how to positively resolve the issue. Hiding it will not make it go away but merely allow it to fester and explode, doing more damage than if it were originally addressed. Generally, semi-structured programs provide the most freedom and the least amount of stress for directors and staff.

A semi-structured program allows for details to be added as needed. It prevents overburdening the director and staff at the onset of the program. The semi-structured programs allow the director, staff and participants to hit the ground running and concentrate on their main purpose, which is the program. The overall vision of the program should be well thought out, but the operational vision can be filled in as need be. Following existing policies within the organization hosting the program will facilitate a more seamless integration of the new program into an existing structure. Semi-structured programs can come into existence in a variety of ways and can develop into fully structured programs if so desired. Semi-structured programs can have a set time limit and can terminate on a positive note. Administrators will have a much easier time finding facilitators among their staff if freedom of operation is emphasized. Administrators need only have a vague overall vision for the program to present it to their staff, which will create a more thorough and well-developed overall vision. Keeping in mind the creative process of individuals, the need for empowerment and ownership will help develop a positive and successful semi-structured program.

4

The Franchise Extracurricular Enrichment Program (or Mind If I Tag Along)

When a new extracurricular enrichment program is introduced into an existing format, this can be considered a franchise program. The new program must conform to the general overall vision and operational vision of an existing fully structured program. The existing structure acts as a guide for future offerings within its program umbrella. A franchise can also be a program or concept demonstrated at a conference to a select group of representatives from a school district or other organization. A new enrichment program can benefit greatly by attaching itself to an already existing set of programs. Though the constraints may limit the creativity and scope of the new program, the stresses of meeting all levels of the fully structured program may be relieved by joining an already established enrichment program. When the concept of a new extracurricular offering arises, it benefits the creators to investigate if there are any existing fully structured programs that they might attach their program to. Getting a new program off the ground and making it successful doesn't require that it exists in a vacuum. The old adage, "there is no need to reinvent the wheel," is very much apropos. Very successful programs

DOI: 10.4324/9781003254911-5

have existed under the umbrella of an already successful set of programs.

Franchise programs offer the creator of the new enrichment activity a set format for designing their program. The overall vision and operational vision of a franchise program must conform to the existing visions of the program housing the new activity. Though there is a limitation on the scope and creativity of the new program, the ease of its assimilation into the existing structure is contingent upon how closely it adheres to both sets of existing visions. A school district or organization may already have a structure in place. My school district put together a long-running afterschool enrichment program set. The lead teachers involved in this created an overall vision and an operational vision and acquired the necessary funding and resources to support a large-scale schoolwide program. This was done with the cooperation of all administrations within the district. The teachers involved in the initial creation of this type of far-reaching enrichment program had previous experience with extracurricular enrichment programs. It will be noted that joining an existing program as a volunteer or other staff member can give future directors and creators insight into the intricacies of designing, creating and maintaining extracurricular enrichment programs.

Large-scale programs do not have to control every detail of each enrichment program housed under its umbrella. Those details will be filled in by the creators of the separate course offerings. When one of these larger fully structured programs exists, creators can focus on content and follow existing operational structures for ease of integration. Most of the time, the content of the program is left up to the director of the program or its creators.

I participated for many years in an existing fully structured extracurricular enrichment program set. The structure of the larger program housing unit was designed in such a way that teachers would write a brief description of their enrichment offering and the participants would select from a group of offerings the ones they wanted. The population of participants was already provided. The resources necessary to facilitate the program were provided. All the schoolwide policies were in effect throughout the program and its franchise programs. All a creator of a new offering had to do was focus on the operations within their own enrichment program. Program choices for participants varied greatly depending on the interests of the teachers facilitating each activity. Offerings such as robot building, cartooning, playing the card game of bridge and many more were available to the participants.

In one such program offered by my district, students were preselected as participants. Criteria for student participation were provided to all teachers within the district. The initial pool of participants came from an already existing category of accelerated students but individual teachers could also nominate non-accelerated students to participate in these enrichment activities. There was a set day and time for each program session. The overall program sessions coincided with the school report card cycle. Students that had violated school rules were unable to participate in the program as a consequence of their actions. A sheet of course offerings and brief descriptions was provided to each participant. The students would select their choices and their alternate choices. The director of the overall program and staff organized the participants and which program they would be assigned. If a program did not have enough student interest, it was dropped much like courses are dropped for the lack of students in a normal school day. The essential snack after school was provided and overall attendance was taken by the main director. The sessions then broke out into individual locations and the students reported to their direct supervisor. Attendance was also taken at the activity's location. The activity had a set time limit and at the end of the overall program, students were dismissed. The operations within the activity were left up to the instructor. The program within my district has existed for over ten years. Though the main director changed the overall vision, the operational vision has stayed through the test of time.

The overall success of this extracurricular enrichment program set is a testament to the viability of franchise programs. The main umbrella program was based on the franchise model. A structure was created to house the various offerings and maintain order throughout the duration of the program sessions.

Creators were given the freedom to choose their activity and the overall operations within their sessions. The program's facilitators merely had to adhere to an existing structure that was very similar to a standard school day classroom. This overall ease and comfort provided for the facilitator gave ample room for creativity and the exploration of ideas and concepts. As the overall program progressed, improvements were made and its strength bolstered. Some extracurricular enrichment offerings became mainstays. The card game of bridge is, to this day, very popular and a constant from the onset of the afterschool enrichment program set. One of the biggest strengths of this type of program is its flexibility for teachers and facilitators to choose new offerings at the end of each multiweek session. This freshness of ideas allowed facilitators to maintain their enthusiasm and desire to impart new knowledge to willing participants.

I learned a great deal about creating and maintaining extracurricular enrichment programs through my experience with another long-standing and well-developed fully structured program. I had been introduced to this program by a college credit offering that integrated teachers into this existing program. The program was started by a professor at the local college. She and her son (also a teacher) took the program from humble beginnings of merely a dozen or so elementary students to a multifaceted complex series of interconnected programs that ran from ages seven to 18. Over 100 student participants came to the two-week, eight hours a day camp every summer. By the time I was involved with it, the program was in full operation. It had morning sessions, a lunch break and afternoon sessions. They had four different categories of participants. The groups were arranged by age and experience level. At the highest level was the apprentice program. At the lowest level was a half-day program geared to younger students. The program brought in art, dance, science, mathematics and language arts. It culminated in a grand performance of an exhibition of student work. The longevity of this program is a tribute to its creators and the well-defined structure that they put in place. I worked with this program as a volunteer and eventually as a franchise program director. My own children participated in this series of programs.

During my volunteer time, I acted as both an impromptu counselor and participant. This experience of full immersion into the activity sessions allowed me to understand the intricacies and nuances of a fully structured program. I learned concepts for the transition from one activity to another. It utilized a grand lens for connecting all activities that participants and staff understood. I experienced the challenges of organizing and empowering others to help create a symbiotic learning community. The scope of this overall program covered the simplest of activities to the most complex performances. The staff consisted of a dozen program specialists and franchise directors and an equal number of college interns. The overall director, my mentor, had covered nearly all contingencies from how the students arrived at the program, what they did during the program's operation and how they would be returned to their respective homes.

The success of a franchise extracurricular enrichment program is directly tied to the overall success of the fully structured program to which it is attached. The strengths of the fully structured program should also be the foundation on which the franchise program is built. If there are weaknesses in the fully structured program, they are going to impact the franchise program. Just like when a rock is thrown into a pond, the ripples it sends out touch all areas of the pond. It is also true that issues that occur in the franchise program will impact the overall fully structured program. This symbiotic relationship must be maintained in order for both programs to prosper. Directors of a franchise program must keep in mind all of the foundational structures of the umbrella program that houses their specific activity. Strong franchises will help the fully structured program grow and prosper. Weak and struggling franchises will limit the overall impact of the fully structured program. When creating a franchise to an already existing program set, the director of the new program must not only create an exciting and dynamic enrichment activity but also adhere to the overall vision and operational vision of the fully structured program that houses the franchise.

The fully structured program may have built into itself a failsafe to guard against franchises that do not meet the criteria of the overall vision of the main program offerings. The more knowledge a new director has regarding the fully structured program will help facilitate the smooth integration of the new franchise. In the two above-mentioned fully structured programs that allowed for franchise programs, their method of dealing with an activity that did not fit within their parameters was the same. Failed franchises were just not supported. In the afterschool enrichment program, lack of participation from the students would indicate failure. If a program lacked the numbers necessary to continue, it would merely be removed from the program offerings. The same would be true for the summer program structure. Every year, the director of the fully structured summer program would put together an agenda and syllabus. If an individual franchised activity was not conducive to the overall program's growth and health, it simply would not be included in that year's selection of activities. Sometimes, a program is too similar to an existing program and the only difference would be the instructor or director. A seniority factor for the programs would then have to be applied. If a prior franchise existed and was in competition with a newer franchise, the new franchise would have to defer to the original program offerings. Sometimes, overall budget constraints can impact the number of activities offered by a larger established fully structured program.

During my tenure with the summer program, I was granted a franchise program. My franchise program was a great success and all participants and staff thought highly of it. Eventually, its timeslot competed with a more senior director's program offering. The funding of the main program limited the number of activities it could support. The director was faced with either lowering all staff's monetary stipend or eliminating some of the activities. I had developed a very strong bond with all the instructors of the existing program and the overall director of the fully structured program. I was not willing to see established members take a cut in pay simply so that I could provide my franchise program. Though it was difficult, I had to defer to the existing more established programs and remove my franchise from the activity offerings. Maintaining this strong bond of existing instructors and programs was more important to me than any money or ability to present an activity. I was given the opportunity to volunteer my time but other challenges piqued my interest and I was sent in a new direction.

Cohesive integration and a near-seamless transition of a franchise program are important for both the fully structured program that houses the activity and the activity itself. A new director must always keep in mind the success of the existing program structure and how their new franchise will add value to the existing programs. The two programs mentioned existed in the same geographic area. The afterschool enrichment program was part of the school district. The summer enrichment program was part of a collaboration between a local college and one of its professors. The proximity of both of these programs allowed for individual teachers, administrators and other stakeholders to observe the original programs and introduce franchise activity concepts.

There is another type of program that allows for franchise opportunities. These types of programs are usually advertised on a national level and/or presented at conferences and workshops. School districts and organizations and their administration and staff can attend these conferences and take part in the presentations. Usually, these types of large-scale franchise-oriented program structures often come with consulting and staff in-service programs. We can call these packaged franchise programs. A packaged franchise program works off an existing structure and overall predesigned set of activities. Schools and organizations wishing to franchise this type of package will be given training on how to incorporate this overall larger concept into their specific school organization.

Administrators in charge of extracurricular enrichment programs get introduced to these types of packaged franchises at statewide or national conferences. Unlike existing fully structured programs that can incorporate local franchises, these packaged franchises come with a fee. Not only does the school district have to pay for the training and materials but also the overall operation of the program. It is not uncommon for an organization seeking to change directions in its operations with student participants to seek out nationally accredited programs to assist in their transition. If a school organization wishes to involve itself in this type of franchise operation, it requires staff and volunteer participation at the onset. Just as it was stated that it is crucial for immersion in existing programs at a local level, these national offerings will require staff to be trained in their overall vision and operational vision. The creativity of its director and staff is limited to the scope of the packaged program. The package program takes away the stresses of creativity of the vision and overall operation structure of the new enrichment activity. Staff merely follow a recipe and adhere to an existing design and educational theory. This type of package program saves time and puts a school district organization on track to create an extracurricular enrichment program in a more expedient manner. Saving time and relieving administrators of the burden of facilitating enrichment programs is one of the main selling points of a packaged franchise. Though the original fully structured program that is now offering franchises may have been extremely successful, there is no guarantee that the success can be replicated by a franchise of the same program. There are never any guarantees that a program will be successful. Some types of franchises have a greater chance of success than others. What makes a program franchised successful and what contributes to its failure is worthy of examination.

What makes a program fail may not be obvious to the program director and the staff. Sometimes, circumstances are beyond the control of the director, staff and organization administrators. Economic changes, population changes or staff changes can impact a program's success. Other reasons for failure can be more obvious. When a franchise fails to meet the overall vision of an existing fully structured program, the probability of the program failing increases dramatically. The first thing a new franchise must embrace is the overall vision of the original fully structured program. The new director and staff must understand what the overall vision entails. This is why I personally recommend full immersion in the original fully structured program before attempting to franchise the activity. My experience as a participant and volunteer contributed to my ability to create a worthwhile, cohesive and easily integrated and successful franchise program. Some programs like the afterschool enrichment program my district offered did not require or need any prior involvement to create a successful program. That type of structure demanded a knowledge of student interests and a connection with the new director's interests.

In the school district's fully structured extracurricular enrichment program framework, a new director needed to be aware of the current offerings of activities and to develop one that did not compete with the already established staff members' programs. If a program was too similar and drew upon the same population, one or both of the programs would suffer. On the other hand, if there was over demand for a type of program, a second offering of a similar program may prove advantageous to the overall enrichment structure. Knowledge of what the students need and what the program would be is important in the development of a new activity. An open dialogue between the fully structured program director and a new franchise director will facilitate successful program development. Generally, the overall vision of the fully structured program must be understood by a new franchise director. The more the new director can embrace the overall vision of the existing program structure, the more cohesive the new activity will be with that existing structure. Maverick directors with their own ideas and visions can meet with difficulty in a franchise structure. The personality and motivation of a new director are factors that can make or break a program's effectiveness. These two traits may be common in the effectiveness of almost any initiative introduced by administration and leadership to faculty and staff. The concept of staff buy-in to any type of program or initiative is the commonality that's present in the introduction of a new extracurricular enrichment program. Packaged programs on a state or national level that bring a new initiative and activity to a school district can have some inherent issues that are more prevalent than if the program was initiated in the local school organization. The problems that a packaged franchise program on a national or statewide level can create stem from the necessary buy-in to the program from staff and faculty.

Conferences and workshops are filled with a variety of vendors and concept presenters. Packaged programs that allow a school district to take an already existing concept and implant it into their own system may seem easier to implement than they actually are. It can also be noted that the chance of failure of these programs is higher than a homebrewed program. What usually happens is a representative of the school district is introduced to a new program concept at a workshop or convention and becomes impressed and wants to implement it in their own home school or organization. The individuals offering this new program will have a set design and structure that must be followed in order for the program to be successful. The initial excitement of the administrator or leadership team about a new initiative may find it difficult to translate that excitement to the necessary faculty and staff required to implement this program. The concept of buy-in dictates the success of these types of initiatives. Whether it's a schoolwide initiative or merely a new more localized activity, without staff buy-in and commitment, the overall success will be very limited. The most successful extracurricular enrichment programs have difficulty transferring that success to other franchises of that program. There are a number of factors that make these packaged franchise programs more difficult to implement than it seems they should be. The reason for these programs' failures may be different in each instance. By looking at several failures that I have witnessed in my years of teaching, we may be able to find a pattern or at least recognize where difficulties can arise.

A member of the school board of my district saw a documentary on a successful extracurricular enrichment program that involved a farmers' market, with a farm providing the vegetables sold at the school-based farmers' market. The original initiative took an eclectic group of students and had them build the stands for the market and work on the farm that produced the vegetables for the market. The original initiative lasted for two years and was quite successful for student involvement, overall enjoyment and the skills that were acquired. Unfortunately, the original program failed due to a lack of funds and external forces opposed to the program. The school board member that had seen the video on the overall concept was so impressed that he wanted to introduce the program into our district. The rudimentary steps necessary to implement this program were put into motion and a committee was formed. The committee consisted of the school superintendent, a building principal, the director of an already existing successful program, the board director himself, several community members and a couple of teachers. I was invited as one of the teachers and as a member of the existing successful program.

The school board director described in detail the documentary he had watched and inspired the members of the committee to pursue a similar program. Several members of the group keyed in on the documentary itself as opposed to the concepts the documentary presented. They joined the school director in insisting that all teachers in the district watch the documentary. From there, ideas flowed about inviting other community members and creating an entire evening event to inspire interest in the new program by viewing the documentary. The rest of the evening was spent talking about how the documentary would be presented. I offered a few comments that perhaps we should focus on what was done and not so much on watching what was done. My suggestion of doing as opposed to viewing did not get support. The concept of having an evening extravaganza and presenting a video documentary was the direction the committee wished to move. The meeting adjourned with the promise that we would meet next week and information would be provided as to the time and place for the documentary to be viewed.

The next meeting came and more members were added to the committee. The superintendent had invited another teacher with experience in video production and two other school administrators. The school board director chaired the meeting and he explained the difficulties he was experiencing acquiring permission to show the documentary to the public. The group was still set on an evening extravaganza and the copyrights and permissions became a sticking point. After much discussion as to why it was so difficult to get the permissions to show the video to the public, the group started discussing plans for their own project. Most of the members had very little concept of what it would take to put together such a program. My mentor, the director of an already successful fully structured program, listened carefully to the committee but offered very little guidance other than encouragement. The discussion came around to what type of project would be utilized to involve the students.

Plans such as growing blueberry bushes and instructing gardening were discussed but no definitive direction was given. The committee seemed to lose energy and focus very quickly. Their initial enthusiasm to show a video and have an extravaganza seemed more important than actually implementing a student-oriented extracurricular enrichment program. Finding that the committee had reached a stalled point, the school board director planned a new committee meeting the next week. At this juncture, I suggested that we concentrate on creating a program instead of presenting a documentary. My mentor perked up at that thought and was willing to help guide the committee in structuring a program. Unfortunately, many of the committee members had keyed in on watching this documentary and felt that it was the single most important element in creating this program. The suggestion that students might be the single most important element in the program seemed to elude some of the members of the committee. I did not attend the third meeting of the committee. I found out later that the superintendent or school principals did not attend and the meeting consisted of the school board director, my mentor and one other teacher. With the inability to acquire rights to show the documentary, the concept fell off the table and disappeared. This failure at the onset of a program gives a glaring example of what not to do.

The concept of the skills-based experiential learning constructivist approach to a program stirred the interests of all members of the initial committee. The amount of work necessary to create that may have been too overwhelming for many of them to comprehend. The familiarity with presenting an evening's program and watching a documentary was well within the comfort zone of many of the members of the committee. Structuring, initiating and participating in an extracurricular enrichment program was not in their comfort zone and therefore something that appeared to be put off until they were more familiar with the concept. Two things played a role in the failure of this initiative. Keying in on one event or item, viewing the documentary, created a loggerhead for moving forward due to a lack of permission to show the video to the general public. The committee got off track and focused on viewing the documentary as opposed to creating the program. The second problem arose when committee meetings became the main focus and not the product of the committee meetings. It was clear that some members of the initial committee preferred just to talk rather than act. The superintendent and other administrators seemed to lack a full understanding of the steps needed to create a new program. The person with the most experience in creating such a program was present as a courtesy and they were only to consult not to create. My mentor, though gracious, had enough on her plate with her existing program and really was only interested in making suggestions that might help the committee create their own program. Getting an initiative out of a committee and onto the drawing board is a challenge. Meeting with people and drawing on other stakeholders is almost essential to the success of a new initiative.

Any administrator, new director or community member that wishes to create a new extracurricular enrichment program needs to be aware of the efficiency needed in running a committee. It seemed that the well-intended school board director did not know what direction he wanted the meeting to go or the extracurricular enrichment program to create. Too much was depending on other members of the committee and not enough details were provided. It is not uncommon to encounter a stumbling block when developing a new program initiative. The creator or initiator must be able to change direction and move the committee of stakeholders toward the goal when a stumbling block is encountered.

There will always be problems and things that must be overcome. Realizing that and having contingencies built into your meeting agenda will prevent this type of morass that traps a wonderful concept in endless committee meetings. The overall purpose needs to be maintained. The overall purpose is the creation of something that will enrich and enhance the lives of the participants. That focus can never be lost. When it is lost the whole concept is lost. The main focus, the acquisition of skills and experiences for students, was derailed by the insistence that a large group of people watch an inspiring documentary. Had the school board director focused on what was going on in the documentary and how it was accomplished and relayed that to the committee members the outcome might have been different. The initial distraction of the drive to present the new initiative derailed the actual program initiative.

It was at this time, I decided to create the Ben Franklin School of Industry. My most successful fully structured program was inspired by the inability of the committee I was involved in to bring fruition to their program. The idea of the skills-based experiential learning constructivist program was exciting to me. In listening to the description of the initial farmers' market documentary, certain concepts were brought forth. Students that participated learned skills. Students that participated learned from their experiences. Students that participated constructed their knowledge from those experiences. This by definition is an experiential learning constructivist approach to education. It is this approach that transforms many extracurricular enrichment programs into dynamic exciting life-changing events for their participants. When a program offers an opportunity for students to experience and utilize new skills, they automatically construct new knowledge and the program becomes successful. Even though the initial documentary explained that the program failed after two years, the reasons for its failure could be avoided in creating a future program. The documentary brought to light what caused the program to fail. The two main issues came from administrative support and budgetary constraints.

Many stakeholders are required to participate if a program of any magnitude is to be established and maintained. The smaller the program, the easier it is to manage, but a large broad program that impacts many students requires a budget and support from several stakeholders. These two factors need to be constantly at the forefront for any director or creator of a large fully structured program. Even with full administrative support and a fully financed budget, a large-scale program is not guaranteed success. My home district was suffering from low teacher morale and low achievement. To make changes that may facilitate improved morale and higher achievement, the school district went in search of programs that they could initiate. Several administrators went to a workshop where this program was presented and they were impressed by its thorough development and success in other districts. Hoping to replicate the same success, the district went about implementing the program. The program was fully staffed and was populated by willing student participants, which had an overall vision and an operational vision with a budget that allowed its full implementation. Still, it did not meet with the success that they had initially hoped it would have.

The program was introduced at a conference and the administrators that were looking for something to increase morale and student achievement found the overall presentation and content of the franchise operation to be the answer to their needs. Upon returning from the conference, the administrators picked the teachers to be involved with the program. They chose the youngest and what they thought were the most enthusiastic teachers. They believed these teachers had the greatest rapport with the students. They then set up a method to select student mentors and lead participants in the program. This was done by a nomination process of all teachers in the school and they selected the students in their classes that they felt had the leadership qualities necessary to help mentor and assist other students. With the staff and the student leaders chosen, workshops were presented for these people. The administrator in charge of the program, which we will now call the director, brought all of the staff together to explain the overall concepts and purpose of the program.

The program was designed to build connections between students and other students and teachers. The goal was to increase both teacher morale and student morale, as well as impact student achievement. It was designed to be a way to bring all of the school population together for the focused purposes of community and achievement. As a sendoff for the program, the entire school was involved in activities. Teacher mentors and student mentors led in these activities and all students in the school were broken up into groups. As the year progressed, more and more connections were to be made and more activities were to be introduced. By the end of the first year, the program suffered a loss of its director, as he was given a higher position in the overall school district. The activities that were planned had to take a backseat to more crucial mandated programs and testing. By the beginning of the second year of the program, it had dwindled and was ineffective. The inability of the program to reach its goals and to be sustained should be examined to understand how these franchises and fully structured programs can collapse in on themselves.

Programs introduced at workshops and conferences are always the best they can be. It is a product and the creators are trying to sell it. When an administration and staff are desperate to make changes in their district, they sometimes grasp at straws. This may well have been the case with my district. The district had in its staff already existing people that could create schoolwide programs and who had created schoolwide programs. They chose to ignore these individuals and any expertise they might have as they struck out to find the solution to their problem. Once they had decided on the franchising of this schoolwide program, they selected the teacher leaders. The method of selection was not one of volunteering but conscripting. Because they chose younger teachers not yet tenured, they were easily able to fill the ranks of their staff. A tenured teacher would need to be convinced that this was a worthy cause. I know from my own experience as a young teacher who was willing to do anything to please my administration and achieve tenure. Though the teachers were young and enthusiastic, their skills in managing and leading students, most especially reluctant students, were limited by their experience. It is a rarity that a young teacher can have a good rapport with the students and maintain a level of leadership and discipline necessary for the highest level of achievement of their students. These skills come in time.

They chose staff they knew would willingly participate in their new initiative but they did not choose staff that could make their initiative successful. Next, they drew upon the student population for their mentors and leaders. They put the task of nominating the students on the shoulders of all of the teachers in the school. Many of the teachers taught the same group of students and the same names came up again and again. Including the underrepresented population, which was one of the goals of this program, was lacking. Many of the students from the underrepresented population did not qualify as mentors or leaders due to grades and behavior. The selection of the student mentors actually created a greater divide between the student body. Many of the mentors were all part of the same peer group and had very little interaction with the underrepresented populations of the school.

During the first schoolwide activity sessions, the overall vision of the program was presented and the operational vision was followed by the teacher and student mentors. The director was present and circulated from activity area to activity area. The student body was broken up into groups to participate in all the activities. It seemed like the most exciting thing for the general student body was the avoidance of regularly scheduled classes. The activities that were planned were not fluid and had issues in the transition from one activity to another. The rest of the year did not see any large-scale group activities just the recognition that there were peer mentors and teacher mentors available to students. Scheduling conflicts prevented further full school activities. When the director took a new position, the transfer of power was not seamless and the new director lacked an understanding of the operational and overall vision. By the second year, it was merely just a statement in the handbook that there were these teacher and student mentors available.

The franchise schoolwide fully structured program did not accomplish what it was supposed to for the following reasons. Conscripting staff as opposed to seeking out willing volunteers was the first mistake. The school lacked a large population of student-oriented teachers. Many of the teachers were more subject oriented. Putting a subject-oriented teacher regardless of their enthusiasm in a student-centered program will most likely not achieve its goals. The student-mentor population, which would be crucial, ended up as a popularity contest. And the student body that was most in need of achievement and morale boosts continued to be underrepresented. The initial structure of how this franchise program was to work did not prove conducive to success. The activity day was not rehearsed. It was planned like most operations within a school—a teacher assigned students

and then assigned an activity. Students with very little experience in leadership were given the job of leading a very large
group of fellow students. The ratio of 30 participating students
to one mentor-student and one mentor-teacher did not meet the
needs of the student participants. There was a difficulty in com-
municating the true purpose of the activities as well as the rules
and the structure of the activities. Though the director circulated
about each activity area, he did not analyze any difficulties and
adjust for them. He merely touched base and let everyone know
he was there and then departed.

The job of the director is far more intensive than that. Even
after the initial rough start, a second activity may have improved
the overall performance of the program. No follow-up programs
were scheduled. In the end, the program only addressed students' needs when the student in need brought them to the attention of a mentor. This reluctance to speak to a peer group or a
teacher is a general attitude of most underrepresented students.
All these factors, and I'm sure more, contributed to the inability
of this program to actualize its goals. Proving that though you
can have all of the necessary resources and funding, there is no
guarantee of success.

Franchise programs can and do work. What seems to be the
most successful type of franchise program is a semi-structured
program that connects to a fully structured established program.
Whether the program is attached directly to a school district
or some other organization, the better run the fully structured
program, the more chance of success its satellite franchise programs have. When a school district wants to undertake a large-
scale fully structured program, there must be an acceptance that
it will be a monumental job. A lot can be learned from analyzing the schoolwide fully structured franchise program described
earlier. One of the biggest contributors to the overall inability of
the program to achieve its planned success occurred when the
original director took another position. Consistency of leadership is important whether it is a single classroom teacher as the
director or a director over a number of staff members. When the
person that initially discovered the franchise program departed
from the scene, the real energy that brought the program to life

dwindled. The person left in charge had not been mentored to be the new director.

Another issue that plagued this burgeoning program was its vastness. There was a large population schoolwide and a single grade level as a focus point was selected. Unfortunately, the size of the single grade population was still unmanageable for the staff and peer mentors. Increasing the number of staff and peer mentors would have alleviated the unmanageable ratio of 30 or more students per teacher and peer mentor. The peer mentors needed more training and should have been more diverse. A suggestion that may have improved the program's overall chances of success would be to focus on the most challenging group.

Reluctant students and noncompliant students impact the school environment whether it is positively or negatively. By focusing on underrepresented populations and reluctant students, the program could have addressed many of the goals it had in its overall vision. As it stood, many of the peer mentors came from the same circle of friends. The unintentional choices of peer mentors by the faculty created that same divide between underrepresented students and popular students. They created the exact thing they were trying to alleviate. These are just some of the situations that arose that caused the program to not achieve what the founders of the franchise expected from this school district. Throughout all these examples of types of programs, we can see that the director plays an intricate role. The director has one of the greatest impacts on the success of the program and their job duties and demeanor are different in many aspects compared with a normal administrator.

5

The Program Director (or Are You Crazy)

Anyone can be the program director for an extracurricular enrichment program and not anyone can be the program director. That's quite a paradox to start the chapter. To understand what it takes to be a successful program director, the whole concept of the job responsibilities and all the intricacies of the position requires exploration. If the body of the extracurricular enrichment program is the student participants it serves, and the blood that nourishes it is the staff, then the program director is both the heart and mind of the whole operation. Someone had to conceive the idea of the extracurricular enrichment program. Someone had to put together the overall package for the program. Someone had to gather the participants for the program. Someone had to get the funding, resources and space necessary for the program. That someone is the program director.

It is true that anyone can wear the mantle of a program director. This mantle comes with a variety of responsibilities and duties. It also requires a certain set of personality traits that often differ from any other administrative leadership position. The program director is the mentor, is the guide, is the ally of all involved and is a servant to the overall success of the program. This stewardship of a burgeoning extracurricular enrichment program is a very demanding responsibility. From my

DOI: 10.4324/9781003254911-6

first extracurricular enrichment program creation to my last, my position as program director became more refined and polished. At the onset of my first endeavor, I fumbled blindly for direction and guidance. I was lucky that the strength of the program and the desire of the student participants in the program were so great. I like a captain of the sailboat with a strong tailwind needed to just steer than propel the program. As I created more and more of these programs, I realized all the necessary qualities that I had to exhibit and the types of challenges I would face. To be the program director of a successful program, one must be able to lead with enthusiasm, drive and determination and follow with cooperation and compassion. By looking at a single session of my last successful program, perhaps we can glean some of the most important responsibilities and attributes a successful program director must possess.

It was 3:30 pm and school had just been dismissed. I went to my car along with three other student participants in the after-school enrichment program known as the Ben Franklin School of Industry. One of those very enthusiastic and wonderful students was in fact, my own daughter. The two other students that rode with me to the facility that housed the program had physical challenges that made it difficult for them to reach the bus stop where the other student participants eagerly awaited to be taken to the program. We drove out of the school parking lot and passed the bus stop where over a dozen other students anxiously waited for the bus to take them to the facility. We arrived at the facility and were greeted by my wife and two volunteers. The volunteers and my wife were both members of a service organization that I also belonged to and were willing to lend their time and energy to prepare the afternoon meal. As soon as I got to the facility, I unpacked the sign-in sheet and placed it at the table at the entrance. All students signed in as they entered the building. Food was being prepared and the tables with the students and staff would eat were set up and ready. My three passengers got their afternoon meal and went to sit at the same table. Eating together is an intricate part of building a learning community. Fifteen minutes had passed and the bus that was to transport the students had yet to arrive. A student participant that drove themselves to the program reported that the remaining students were still at the bus stop waiting.

A phone call to the bus company that had provided this service was made. The dispatcher at the bus company assured us the bus was coming. It was late due to a prior commitment. A phone call was made to one of the lead students at the bus stop by my daughter. My daughter had taken the role of peer leadership in the program. She called and assured the students the bus was coming and to wait patiently for the transportation. Within five minutes, the other students had arrived and gathered their food and sat down at the various tables to eat. One of the newer students to the program sat by themselves.

Seeing their immediate isolation from the general body of the students participating, I instructed a pair of students that were eating at a table to invite the other student to join them or to join that other student at their table. I reminded the veteran students that it is this welcoming camaraderie that everyone in the program enjoys. With everyone eating with someone and no one alone I went about the other organizational tasks. The college interns assisting in the program arrived and I directed them to get a meal and handed them the day's agenda. As the students finished their meal, the teacher volunteers arrived. I met with each volunteer individually and discussed this session's goals and their assignments. The teacher volunteers also ate with the body of students. I then directed various student groups to their teacher mentors for that day's activities.

Some students would be going on a nature walk with a local environmentalist while another group of students worked on a series of experiments with wind turbines. Another group of students worked on the construction of a 3D printer. The remaining students participated in the building's library and meeting room for a discussion of economics with my friend and department chair of the economics department of the local college. Everyone was instructed that students would transition from one activity to the next at 45-minute intervals. Each teacher instructor had prepared for their activity and took charge of the four to six students that were assigned to their session. The length of the program allowed for two 45-minute sessions.

The students and their mentors broke off and went to their respective activities. I checked on the food service volunteers and they were packing up any leftovers for students to take with them at the end of the program session. I graciously thanked the two volunteers and my wife. At this point, I will impress upon everyone how much of an ally and an assistant my wife proved to be throughout the life of the Ben Franklin School of Industry. In group leadership seminars, it is often mentioned that a leader requires a dedicated first follower. Someone who gives their all and believes wholeheartedly in the vision of the leader and the purpose of the program. Without a shadow of a doubt, my first follower was my wife, and without her help, the program would have not been the success it was. The two ladies that had volunteered to prepare the food departed and my wife started to circulate to the various groups within the building to see if there was anything they needed. I also began circulating. Each group had different needs and when I arrived at their meeting area, I was greeted with smiles from both the students and the teacher volunteer.

The teacher volunteer had a list of things that needed to be done or addressed and gave them to me. Those demands that I could immediately address I did and the others that required resources outside of what we possessed I would have to acquire. I spent roughly five minutes with each group and then moved on to the next area. After all the program activities housed within the building were checked, I began the long trek to the outdoor activity area. I found the environmentalist and his group of students immersed in the exploration of the various plants and insects in the outdoor learning area. I stayed with them until it was time to transition to the next activity.

As our group made our way back through the semi-wetland environment, one student that had mobility issues fell into the mud. I was still dressed in my teaching attire. Seeing the embarrassment that the student was experiencing having been the only one to fall in the mud, I immediately accidentally slipped and fell completely into the mud and covered myself and had difficulty getting up to my feet. All the students smiled and chuckled; any attention on their peer who had initially fallen was completely forgotten and the fact that their director was now a mud puppy was far more entertaining. Did I deliberately fall in the mud? Of course, I did. As we made our way back to the facility, the other groups were ready to transition. Students were lined up waiting to go on the nature walk while other students were greeted by the mentor of the next activity. I gathered the groups together and made sure that everyone was accounted for and the second part of the day's session commenced.

As the time to end this day session approached, I double-checked the participants and the materials and prepared for dismissal. Some students left via their parents, other students were transported by the bus company and my wife and I transported the remaining students to their homes. Before we departed the facility, every participant made sure their areas were clean and that the facility was just the way they found it at the beginning of the session. Each student that departed was accounted for, those that remained helped to close up and checked for any lights that were on, materials that were left out and bookbags or phones that were forgotten. Leftovers were eagerly taken by the students to be shared with their family members when they got home. An hour after the program ended, I finally arrived at my home and could rest.

As the director of the Ben Franklin School of Industry, I culminated my experience in creating and maintaining successful extracurricular programs. This single snapshot of the session of the overall program can give us all insight into the overall duties and responsibilities of a program director. Though the overall vision of the program was not mentioned in the narrative, the presence of its overarching influence can be seen. One of the biggest components of the overall vision for the program was building skills. Interpersonal skills and physical skills are basic requirements for the achievement of any goal. The operational vision of the program influenced every moment the program was active. It is this operational vision and its implementation where the responsibilities and duties of the director can be defined. We see the problems and challenges facing a program throughout a single session. The Ben Franklin School of Industry was a fully structured program with multiple mentors and learning groups.

At any single session, the population of student participants could exceed 20.

The duty of knowing who is present and where they are throughout the term of the session was at the very foundation of the program's success. Attendance and knowledge of the whereabouts of students coming into the program facility allowed for all of the rest of the operation and activities to occur fluidly. This skill for a director would be similar to classroom management. Transportation became an issue in the small vignette and is quite an issue for all programs. Getting participants to and from the program facility is crucial. Whether the students are staying in their home school or are reporting to another location within the community, how they get there safely is the director's responsibility. The director must be able to arrange transportation to and from the program location. If a program director leaves the transportation issue up to the student participants, they may find the students might not be as diligent or punctual as the program's operational vision requires. An ability or knowledge of community resources is invaluable for a director. Meals for any extended day program must be considered. Many underserved students deal with hunger issues. These issues need to be addressed in a manner that makes all participants comfortable and allows for interaction among the participants. The larger the program, the more effort is required on the part of the director to provide nutrition.

Volunteers are another important part of the successful program equation. I relied on three volunteers, two of which were strictly dedicated to food services. The third acted as not only a food service worker but a full-fledged mentor involved with circulating around all parts of the program and interacting with the participants and staff. These three individuals made the meal portion of the program welcoming and friendly. Student participants were instructed on how they would be served by the three volunteers. Ensuring that all students got to eat and were not left alone while eating became both the staff's and the participant's responsibility. Building camaraderie and a sense of community need to be in a program director's skill set. Before the actual activity portion of the program session began, the director created a smooth transition from a standard school day to the enrichment program.

Keep in mind that the overall purpose of the program is the enrichment of the student participant's life. Every student regardless of their academic standing deserves and benefits from enrichment. Acquiring enough interest in the program was a requirement before any of the standard operations could occur. A successful director needs to be able to bring people together and create interest in their program. They also need to be able to recognize when potential programs are formed by student interest. The students that need enrichment opportunities the most are the least likely to receive them. It always serves a program well to be extremely inclusive. Reluctant learners are not likely to participate in any program offered by a school and perhaps other organizations. The ability to recruit viable candidates to participate in the program and contribute to its success is yet another attribute a program director must possess.

Good coaches have the ability to see talent and potential and then convince the athlete to participate in their sport. It might be said that a successful program director is much like a successful coach. Sometimes merely advertising the opportunity will attract a number of participants to make the program viable, especially if the focus of the program is of high interest to a large number of students in the school. If the program populates quickly, the program director must save for future growth and interest. Underserved students may not at first show interest in becoming part of the program population. The program director may have to reach out and make access to the program more personalized. Knowing each student participant and interacting with each and every one of them at every session is important in several aspects. Circulating throughout the activities during the session time allows the program director opportunities to interact and gain a better understanding of the staff and participants. Being able to interact with staff and bring out their best performance increases the program's chances of success exponentially.

It is this part of the director's duties and responsibilities that differentiates a program director from a standard school or organizational administrator. An extracurricular enrichment program director most likely has a staff of volunteers and modestly compensated professionals. How these adults feel about the program, the participants and the director impact all aspects of the program. Not only must program directors choose the right staff members but they must also encourage and guide them in the direction of the program's overall vision. A program director must lead from the front and support from the rear. They have to do this simultaneously. Volunteers need to feel comfortable, welcome, appreciated and respected. Program directors must make sure that each volunteer feels integral to the overall program success. These interpersonal skills should be openly modeled for all members of the enrichment program. A program director must serve as a resource provider and have answers and suggestions that are positive and productive. It may be difficult for a full-time administrator to transform into that type of position. Leadership styles can vary but a program director's leadership style should be more consistent with the cordial host and willing servant.

The affinity that a program director should nurture with their staff may not fit into the daily operations of a school. When an administrator shows up at a classroom door, the majority of the population of the room has some degree of uneasiness. If some of the student participant population have behavioral issues inside the normal school day, they may not interact naturally due to the presence of an authority figure. This doesn't mean it isn't possible for a full-time administrator to direct an enrichment program. One of my other key mentors throughout my educational career was an administrator of the highest levels throughout schools and universities. She didn't become a director of a very successful extracurricular enrichment program until after she retired from full-time administration. She was able to become more matronly and nurturing because of her freedom from the direct leadership of teachers and staff. There are distinct differences in the leadership of an extracurricular enrichment program and leadership inside a classroom, or leadership of an entire school or organization. All types of leadership are challenging and require the ability to maintain a position of authority and yet a position of cooperation.

The program director must be stronger in the cooperative sense than the authoritarian. Unlike organizations with hired staff, the extracurricular enrichment program usually involves modest stipends or complete volunteerism. Individuals familiar with organizational and school leadership may have difficulty working with volunteers. School principals have an aura of authority by position regardless of disposition. Volunteers only operate within the bounds of the leader's authority as long as their comfort level is not infringed upon. Ordering around volunteers is probably the easiest way to lose a volunteer. Heavy-handed authority does not mix well with a cooperative atmosphere. Moving from the position of authority in a workplace to a position of authority within a voluntary program can be difficult for some administrators. Moving from a position of following directions to one of giving directions can be difficult for individuals not in leadership positions. Classroom teachers have authority over the students that enter their classroom and populate the school during the standard school day, but beyond that, their authority can be questioned. Authority by position in an extracurricular enrichment program does not truly exist.

All participants come willingly to the program and can just as easily exit the program. It only takes one incident of anger on the part of the leader to taint the entire program. My experience with leadership as a foreman or department manager differed greatly from any other leadership position I have held. As I was interning as a school administrator, I observed a number of different leadership styles from the implementation viewpoint. My administrative mentors' leadership styles differed from one another, but both had an authoritative air to it that was granted by position rather than earned by reputation. With the exception of my number one mentor in my educational career, I have not observed a leadership style that is conducive to acting as a program director as long as the individual administrator was still in authority within their school district. My mentor still had that air of authority but had earned that authority by a reputation of hard work, diligence, community involvement and direct impact on people in education. If an administrator has those qualities, then they are well-equipped to pursue program directorship of an extracurricular enrichment initiative.

This is not to say that the school administrator or district administrator cannot create the overall vision and the operational vision of an extracurricular enrichment program. It might well fall upon the shoulders of the building administrator to create a fully structured program. Most likely, such an administrator is already overwhelmed with duties and obligations. It is here that the administrator must select the perfect individual to expedite their vision. A number of times various building administrators came to me and asked me to undertake the leadership of a semi-structured extracurricular enrichment program. As I've stated before, a cordial working relationship with school administration is essential for success in teaching and other school-related activities. Adversarial attitudes have no place in a school. Disagreements with the administration have a specific process that must be followed. Administrators wishing to select a director to fit the vision to their enrichment program must be as judicious as selecting an individual to fill a teaching position.

An administrator needs to pair both the vision of the enrichment program and the individual that will direct in such a manner that both prosper. If the fit of the program and the choice of directors is not well matched, neither the director nor the program are going to be successful. One hint that may work to find that perfect director may be to just talk to the staff about the vision in small groups or as individuals and get their take on it and gauge their interest. The adage of if you want something done find a busy individual may be true, but the demands of the program director may be too great for such an individual. Perhaps, a teacher that has a history of successful student rapport and may have stepped down from a coaching position or some other activity might be more suitable. Finding someone who's hungry for the challenge would be an excellent choice. Sometimes new teachers can be excited to do such a program but may require a knowledge base they do not possess. Hence, one of the purposes of this book, as stated at the beginning of this chapter, anyone can be a program director.

An enthusiastic individual with creativity and drive can be guided by an administrator to become a superb enrichment program director. I strongly stress empowerment. The more empowered I felt by my administration, the more effort and energy I put toward endeavors that benefited the school and students. An administrator cannot have a loose cannon on their staff without fear of grievous errors being made. An administrator must hold the reins of highly energetic and creative individuals in such a manner as to direct but yet let their enthusiasm drive the process. The invisible hand of an administrator will be greatly successful in the creation of an extracurricular enrichment program directed by an enthusiastic energetic young teacher. Veteran teachers can be included or encouraged to take on these endeavors if their interests and the overall vision coincide. Igniting the fire of an old dog can be just as rewarding as guiding a novice teacher. Administrators must believe that within their staff is an individual that will make the vision of an enrichment program come to life. If, by chance, an individual outside of the school has the talent, skills and motivation to take on the job of program director, they too may be a perfect fit. If they are on the staff already, individuals that create afterschool programs may offer up opportunities to create a far greater overall enrichment program. Though the school day and beyond is often very challenging and demanding for an administrator, having knowledge of their staff's activities after hours can sometimes be beneficial.

My administrators became aware of the Impossible Dream Machine's operation via word-of-mouth and simply walking the school after hours. The working relationship I developed with them and they developed with me allowed for an ease of integration into the operations of a daily session of my enrichment program. Their knowledge of the student body and their individual idiosyncrasies allowed them to see the potential of the program. The only thing they had to do to bring the program into the umbrella of their extracurricular activities was to support it with positive accommodations and minor resources. The program allowed them to interact in a way that they found refreshing. Empowering the teacher who has taken the steps to create something wonderful for students benefits the school, the administrators and the community. The level of staff awareness possessed by the administrator will directly impact their ability to recruit the necessary individual for the position of program director. Overburdened administration may not have the luxury of a full understanding of their staff. The operations of the school they lead may act as a detriment in their ability to find and promote successful extracurricular enrichment programs and the directors of those programs.

Some general guidelines that may assist in the search for the program director that will bring success to a vision of an extracurricular enrichment program can prove helpful to all administrators, especially those that are hard-pressed for time. Enthusiasm and interest are two key components that a candidate for program director must possess. A brief conversation with individuals about overarching concepts that would be encompassed in a program can often lead to hints of interest in the program. Being able to recognize something that ignites the fire of an individual teacher is key to the administrator's search. Administrators are by nature talent scouts. They staff their entire organization or school with individuals who they find to have the talent necessary to complete the overall picture of the educational institution they lead. Building a new extracurricular enrichment program whether it is a single classroom or multi-classroom size is a task that should be delegated. Once an administrator finds the spark that ignites the individual teacher, there are still other checkboxes that need to be addressed to determine if the teacher is capable of bringing this new enrichment opportunity to fruition. The organizational demands of a program director are an aspect of the skill set the prospective candidate must possess. If the candidate is too haphazard and careless with their organization of the classroom and other activities, then that will transfer directly to the enrichment program. If the candidate is too rigid and structured, their organizational skills may be exemplary but the ability to move fluidly from one transition to another inside the extracurricular enrichment program may be compromised. It is a delicate balance between creative genius and obsessive compulsion that guides the successful program director. If an adequate number of organizational skills is present in the candidate, there are still other very important attributes they must possess in order to increase the probability of the program's success.

That all-important rapport with the students must be present throughout the candidate's overall daily classroom leadership. Teachers that create effective learning communities will also create effective enrichment programs. The candidate does not need to be the best friend of their students, but there must be this connection that is stronger than just a temporary sharing of a room and subject content. Student-oriented teachers are the best candidates for the role of program director. Subject-oriented teachers may suffer a deficiency in the student rapport department. The effectiveness of the teacher in the classroom can be an indication of their effectiveness in an enrichment program. Just because a teacher has never been part of an extracurricular activity does not exclude them from the leadership of a new endeavor. It is this novice individual that brings a new vision and perspective to an undertaking. Choosing a novice as the program director for a new enrichment initiative will require that the administrator mentors and provides reassurance and assistance as the project progresses. A novice teacher may be enthusiastic and willing to take on the task but they may lack some of the subtleties that make such programs successful. Imparting knowledge and experience will be both welcomed and appreciated by the novice program director. Even if the teacher undertaking the program directorship is a veteran, they may still require encouragement, resources and mentorship from the administrator that wishes to see the overall vision of this extracurricular activity be successful. Veteran teachers will have different demands than novice teachers when it comes to the implementation of these types of programs. With a veteran, the management skills and leadership ability are already present, but they may lack the experience to bring an overall vision and operational vision of a program into a synergistic dynamic. The synergistic dynamic that an enrichment program provides differentiates it from a standard course offering during the school day. The successful enrichment program will incorporate the individual participant's energy and enthusiasm and the vision and enthusiasm of the project director and their staff.

A hybrid version of program director may be a solution to a situation where a novice teacher is excited to take on the challenge of a new program but lacks the depth of skills necessary to ensure success. Partnering the novice with a veteran teacher may prove advantageous. A veteran teacher that has too many external demands to dedicate themselves as a full-time project director may be able to act as an assistant and mentor to a novice teacher that is willing to take the helm of leadership. The reassurance of having a veteran to assist the neophyte should enable the program to get underway and be steered toward success. If a dynamic friendly work relationship exists between the veteran and the novice, the program's success greatly increases. The unintended consequences may prove to be beneficial to both the veteran and the novice. Sometimes, a veteran teacher will not commit to a full-time extra responsibility but will act as a resource and an extra hand for both the novice program director and the administrator that envisions a successful extracurricular enrichment program.

6

On Being the Program Director (or You Knew the Job Was Dangerous When You Took it)

For all those contemplating or having already accepted the mantle of program director of a new extracurricular enrichment program, the information within this chapter will give you some insights and hopefully direct guidance on how to accomplish this undertaking. There are many things to consider once you've decided to be the program director. Some may seem more important or more challenging than others and that is normal with almost any undertaking. A program director of this type of enrichment offering is a different type of administrator than any other within the sphere of a school or an organization. Because this is a new undertaking, many uncharted waters must be crossed. Each program will have its differences that make it unique to your school and student participants. There are similarities in program structures with other existing programs and depending on whether it is a grassroots, semi-structured, franchised, or fully structured program, the demands will increase as the structure is defined.

A prospective program director needs to consider the demands that will be placed upon him or her. Leadership at the initial start of this type of program has some key components that

DOI: 10.4324/9781003254911-7

need to be at the forefront of a director's thoughts. The time and energy for creating, launching and maintaining an enrichment program must not be downplayed. The only set defining rules of these types of programs may only come from this book. Any successful extracurricular enrichment program is often a creation of the imagination of the individuals that envisioned it. A student's need for enrichment is the main reason such programs form. The stewardship of something as impacting as an enrichment program requires constant reflection and modification to the program and its operations. To accomplish a successful program initiation and to continue its operation, specific challenges are placed in front of a prospective or existing program director.

Time and energy are very tangible challenges that must be immediately understood and addressed by the program director. The amount of time required to operate a successful program is as demanding as any other extracurricular activity provided for students. My most successful and final fully structured program achieved its goals with the help of many people but most especially the help of my family. My daughter's participation and my wife's volunteerism helped ensure the success of my dream and vision. The time commitment, a quality enrichment program requires, cannot jeopardize the time commitment and quality given to your family. Family first is a mantra that must be adhered to by anyone wanting to create something so enriching and life-changing for all participants. Jeopardizing your family for the success of a program will not accomplish the success of the program nor the success of the family. Many of my programs were initiated and operated while I was unmarried. Others just as successful existed during my marriage. I was grateful for the time allotted to the programs from my family and their involvement in any way to help assist in the program's successes. A program director without too many family challenges will have a less stressful experience whether the program director is young and has yet to start a family or is older and has a well-established family that requires less time commitment. Retired teachers and administrators sometimes have the greatest amount of time to dedicate to these types of programs. Unfortunately, I find myself in retirement and not sure that I have the energy to devote to creating a new program. Energy is going to be another premium item a program director must possess.

The energy demands of a burgeoning program may seem daunting but the energy demands of maintaining and funding an ongoing program can be equally as daunting. If a prospective program director is not in good health, the energy demands may be far too great, jeopardizing their health as well as the program. The program director has got to be health conscious. As important as maintaining a good healthy family, maintaining a good healthy body is an equally important aspect of the job. The program director must always show enthusiasm and energy. It may be absolutely necessary if the program hits a low point and pivots toward diminished results. The program director will have to dig deep into their willpower and produce the energy and enthusiasm necessary to bring the program out of the doldrums it may have found itself in. All programs will have their ups and downs but a program director cannot have ups and downs. At best, a program director can have ups and plateaus. It is much easier to summon the energy to move to a new level rather than summon the energy to pull the program out of a nosedive. The program director is a constant source of positive encouragement and guidance throughout the life of the program. There is no downtime for the program director during the operation of the session.

At the onset of each session, students and staff joined in meals and reenergized themselves for the program ahead but as program director I had to eat on the run. The responsibilities of a successful session launch and its proper management pulled me in many directions. Each direction had to be addressed with an equal amount of attention. Seldom did I find a moment's peace to gather my thoughts and catch my breath. Constant motion is the nature of the position during the session's operations. It is only when all participants have been safely delivered to their homes and the program is at rest that the program director can also be at rest. This time at rest must be devoid of stresses and worries of the continuation of the program. A program director must shed all responsibilities and thoughts during the time of rest. Without quality rest, the energy and thought processes required to keep a successful enrichment program on track will be jeopardized.

Time and energy are two key components that must be possessed by a prospective program director. The demands on a program director will vary in degree and intensity as the program moves to a fully structured entity. The more structured the program becomes, the more demands placed upon individuals that are operating the program increase. Organizational skills are another aspect that a program director must possess. Each person differs in how they organize their thoughts and how they organize their actions. What method works for one person may not be workable for another. Some people keep a lot of information in their head while others write it down step-by-step. A program director has to find a comfort level with organizing to operate a successful program. The need for organization cannot be denied but how individuals create their organization is a matter of preference.

Each type of program differs in the type of demands of organization. Some standards have to be adhered to and accomplished successfully in order to ensure overall program success. Attendance and knowledge of the whereabouts of all participants, as has been stressed, are crucial to the overall success of the programs. The operational vision of an enrichment program should guide the level of structure required. Some programs require just attendance and a few resources to conduct the program. A program like a card game activity might just require the program director to teach the game and facilitate play. A culminating goal of a card game activity might be a competition. There is a requirement for organization that cannot be ignored. Something as simple as a competition will require some type of structure in order for it to occur seamlessly. If the program has several activities included within the session, organizing transitions and time will be very important. Time management for the operation of the session may require an agenda and or some other structures to guide participants and staff toward the end goal. The end goal of the program will impact the level of structure required during the program's sessions.

In creating a magazine, organizational skills are at peak demand from the program director. Though the Impossible Dream Machine was a grassroots-formed enrichment program, the product of the magazine could not have occurred without deadlines and resource management. With most enrichment programs, resources may be at a premium. A program director may be limited in funding and resources. Meeting the end goal requires the program director to be aware of the available resources and the funds to purchase further resources. If a magazine cover is to be printed on card stock, the program director must ensure that there is an adequate amount of card stock to print all of the proposed magazines. Using resources for purposes not originally designated can lead to shortages. Students, as well as some staff, may not have a full grasp of the limitations of the resources of the program. Resources can unknowingly be diverted and expended. Such an event occurred with the magazine we were trying to produce. The cover stock was bright fluorescent orange and green. Some students became fascinated by the color of the paper and chose to draw on it rather than save it for the printing process. The concept of black and white photocopies was not in some of my students' thought processes. They had completed some wonderful artwork and writing on the brightly colored paper and wanted to include their work in the final product. The need to work strictly on white paper with black text and lines was not stressed enough and I was faced with the sad duty of explaining that the work would not reproduce. This brings us to another aspect program directors must consider. When working toward an end product or goal, there will be times when various members of the learning community get disheartened and frustrated. This can occur in staff and participants.

A program director sometimes has to be a morale officer. Coaches find themselves in this position whenever their team is losing or a player has failed at their job. It is not unusual for teachers to experience this if a student gets a low test score and wants to give up. The difference in extracurricular enrichment programs and all other aspects of education centers around the desire to participate. If a student loses the desire to participate, they may impact the entire program. Disillusionment and disenchantment can occur, especially if expectations are too unrealistic on the part of the participant or the staff. Keeping expectations high yet grounded in reality can help prevent disillusionment.

When a student loses their desire to participate in the program, the director is faced with another unplanned circumstance. The program director must determine if the student is not a correct fit for the program and therefore leaving the program is advantageous to both the student and the program.

The program director must determine if this is a temporary feeling that occurred through some event in the program or a permanent attitude. When a student is working on something and it doesn't manifest in the way that they had planned, it may cause them to be disappointed and frustrated. This is not unusual throughout any educational experience. How the program director addresses this will be important for the overall health and welfare of both participants and the program. The concept of enrichment must permeate the entire program. Enriching the lives of all the participants is an unwritten goal. When a participant is disillusioned and wants to leave the program or withdraw from the program but still be part of it, the program director must address this situation correctly.

In a classroom setting, a teacher has more options on how to handle reluctant learners and disenchanted students. At the very end, if nothing works to encourage and bring them out of their doldrums, the grade is what the grade is. Though every teacher wants all students to succeed, it is not always the case. With an extracurricular enrichment program, the success of the student is part of the success of the program. If one student fails to achieve the goal, then part of the success of the program has failed to achieve its goal. Each member of the learning community that creates the enrichment program needs to somehow move forward and become enriched by the program and its goals and products. Students that become disenchanted or discouraged bring special demands on a program director. There is no one solution for encouraging the discouraged.

Several avenues can be pursued but each one is almost up to the individual program director to discover. Sometimes encouraging words will work. Sometimes assisting in the completion of a task that is frustrating the student or changing the task may be the solution. There is no panacea for disillusioned and frustrated students that participate in an enrichment program. There is, however, a need for dogged determination on the part of the program director to see that students succeed. The determination to not give up on a student may be actually all the student needs to pick themselves back up and begin participating in the program again. As the director, a person must be aware of the importance that all students achieve. That may be a classroom goal but it must become an enrichment program reality. The very makeup of the student body that participates in these programs may be part of the solution. Sometimes peers can succeed when authority figures fail. The population of the participants is another point prospective program directors must consider.

Merely posting what the program is or announcing it on the loudspeaker may not draw all the necessary participants. Underserved populations are often reluctant to risk involvement in anything extracurricular. Their school day may be filled with trauma and stress. They may believe that the extra activity is just one more chance to get hurt. The initial group of students that want to take part in the program is just the beginning of the population of the program. Enrichment is for the gifted and the challenged and everyone in between. When an inclusive program exists, enrichment for all demographics of the school population can occur. The enrichment program sometimes requires the recruitment of both highly skilled students and students in need of a first-time enrichment experience. The program director must be a talent scout. This is not to say that you're only looking for highly skilled students to populate your program, but, in fact, you're looking for the correct type of student that will benefit from the program.

Not all enrichment programs fit a student's desires or needs and trying to force student participation in an activity that they are just not interested in, and have no attachment to, most often ends in disappointment for all involved. Having that overall vision of what enrichment is going to be provided for the student population and all members of the learning community is the starting point of your recruitment efforts. Recognizing student talent and student interest requires good observation skills and an open-minded perspective. Effective program directors can see within the student what would interest and benefit them.

Students most often do not recognize their own potential. The concept of enrichment is to exceed the potential. When a student participant has never really tried in academic settings, enrichment settings or any other scholastic venue, even the slightest improvement can be monumental in their life. A student that has achieved greatness without the program is much harder to enrich than a student who has experienced disappointment, frustration and defeat throughout their academic career. It is this student that benefits immensely from the program and gives the program its true value. A program should at its very heart be transformative for all that participate.

With the transformative concept as a key purpose of the enrichment program, finding the right mix of participants will assist in the overall success the program wishes to achieve. With a grassroots self-starting program, the students are drawn to it, and through word-of-mouth, they connect their friends and students that are interested in the product and goal of the program. The program director works with this type of group to bring them into a cohesive functioning organization. With a semi-structured program, the population of participants may already be there to draw upon and their mutual interest may bring them quickly into a well-functioning learning community. The franchise program can draw the correct population but there is more chance that the program may not be successful due to the size of the population that participates. If the franchise program is a small classroom size population not exceeding a ratio of ten students to one adult mentor, the chances of success greatly increase. As illustrated before, a grade-level program may have too many participants that do not have the program's overall vision and goals at the forefront of their involvement.

With a fully structured program, a program director will have the greatest control of the demographics and student participants that will populate the program. Fully structured programs already have a predetermined number of students that can participate and often a specific type of student that will be best served by the enrichment program. An optimum mix of highly skilled dedicated students and inexperienced students can provide amazing results. It might only take the recruitment of one very highly skilled and motivated student to help establish a successful program. Including more of these highly motivated students increases the probability of success of the overall program. Peer mentorship is another important part of a true enrichment program. The rewards for all involved when peer mentorship and a solid positive learning community are established cannot be overstated. Understanding the key ingredients of the students and the appropriate mix of skills and interests creates a nice atmosphere to develop these types of programs. If the program involves other adults, the program director must be very judicious in selecting the correct individuals that will act as mentors and guides for the program.

A potential program director needs to have a cordial and respected reputation among colleagues. The more programs the leader is involved with or has been involved with will impact the level of respect granted to them by their colleagues. The very nature of a teacher is one of helping students to reach or exceed their potential. Hopefully, in searching for assistance, there should be if not an abundance at least an ample number of potential volunteers or modestly paid staff. The extracurricular enrichment program is not a get-rich-quick scheme. At best, it is a modest stipend that allows the staff some financial benefit. It would be wonderful if a program director found individuals of a like mindset and in lockstep with their vision. This would be ideal. It is, however, not always the case. When searching for adult members of the program, the overall vision and goals of the program need to be clearly defined.

Vague and ambiguous visions and goals will not lend themselves to attracting the correct mentors. Disorganization and poor leadership skills will also detract from selecting valuable members to help lead the program. All staff members must share the overall vision of the program. If they do not share this vision, they will be unable to bring students to the successful level of achieving the goals of that vision. Selecting the correct adult mentors for the enrichment program is just the beginning of the director's involvement with the staff. Just like the interactions with the student participants, the director must have steady and consistent interactions with the staff. The program director must be able to be there when the staff are frustrated or lacking something. One gauge of the success of a program director's leadership is when in circulating throughout the session, each staff member has a smile, perhaps a joke and some request that the leader can fulfill.

In choosing staff, a knowledge of how they feel and interact with each other is important. Major goals of the program can help draw in staff members to work in cooperation for the overall achievement and success of the program. When a staff member feels that they are an integral part of the program's success they are more likely to give their full energy and enthusiasm toward the goal. If a staff member feels taken for granted or overburdened, they will be resistant to continuing as a volunteer or even a paid member. Oftentimes, the gratitude and appreciation for their time and their knowledge are provided by the students they are involved with and this is another key part of a successful program.

When the staff themselves feel that they are making significant contributions to the enrichment and improvement of every student that they are interacting with, their zeal for the success of the program can match that of the program director themselves. Having both an inclusive demographic of student participants and dedicated mentors, a solid growing learning community and enrichment program can be established. The nuts and bolts of operating a larger program involving other adults will require resource management and acquisition. Fundraising at the onset may fall solely on the shoulders of the program director.

Not only will funds be necessary but perhaps equipment and materials will assist in the program's overall success. The establishment of the overall vision and the operational vision is integral in the acquisition of funds, resources and materials. A potential program director may have a vision of the enrichment activity but not an understanding of how to find and gather resources. Strong working relationships with the school administration or administrators from different organizations are fundamental for this process to occur. The maverick program director had best be well connected with entities outside of the school or organization if they are to do this alone. This is not a recommended method.

Once the overall vision has been established and an understanding of how the program will operate is defined, the program director can pursue assistance from the administration. School administrators have many resources. A district's curriculum director may be the most valuable connection a potential enrichment program director can establish. It is recommended that this positive interaction with a curriculum director should already exist. I was blessed with a number of very cooperative curriculum directors throughout my career. My reputation for creating programs and positive interaction with the students proceeded me. My curriculum directors received my ideas in a positive light and were often able to assist in refining the overall and operational vision of the program. During the life of my fully structured program, a physical education component was included. My friendship with a retired gym teacher provided me the opportunity to enlist his services. The school had ceased to provide archery as an elective physical education subject. My school principal willingly provided all of the unused archery equipment for the program. Having acquired valuable material at no cost whatsoever was an exceptionally beneficial event. Having the equipment necessary to provide archery lessons and an individual who found archery lessons to be rewarding, and something they missed on their retirement, gave a component to the program that was irreplaceable.

The majority of the population of the program were urban students and the chance to learn archery was infectious and infatuated them. That joy in the eyes of the instructor as the students all improved and got bull's-eyes is something I hold in my memory to this day. This is an example of how with only a modest stipend, which my teacher friend did not require or expect, and the assistance of a school administrator providing unused resources contributed to the overall success of the students, staff and program. Fundraising and resource gathering are so crucial to an expansive and inclusive enrichment program that those concepts merit an entire chapter dedicated to themselves. The skill set a potential program director must have is not just limited to the topics discussed in this chapter. The many hats a program director must wear are dependent on the program's vision and operation. Community relations may be something that a classroom teacher has not considered as important to an extracurricular enrichment program.

The community in which the school district operates has a vast array of potential stakeholders, resource providers and program funding. Local businesses and community organizations can be far more helpful than someone new to program directing can realize. It is easier for someone who is already involved with the community to reach out to potential stakeholders. If the potential program director does not live within the community, these connections may be difficult to make. Living within the community, the teacher or director adds an extra component that is beneficial to program initiation and longevity. Connections in the community do not occur overnight. If the program director lacks community connections, reaching out to friends and associates that do may prove helpful. School administrators tend to have stronger community connections and it may be their assistance in this department that helps the program director connect the enrichment activity with the community.

Having a fleshed-out overall vision and a comprehensive operational vision will help in garnering community support. Keep in mind that other established student programs have already reached out to many community members. Programs similar to those that already exist will find it harder to gain stakeholders that are not already attached to more established programs. The more unique and connected it is to the stakeholder the program director is petitioning for aid, the more likely the program will receive it. My fully structured program reached out to an agricultural entrepreneur. When he was informed of the wetlands component of the overall program, his interest in teaching environmental science was engaged. His interest in imparting his knowledge of the environment of the area created an aspect of the program that was only partially conceived at its inception. The skills this one volunteer brought the program added a new dimension that provided an immersion in nature that many urban students had never experienced. The community and its members may be surprising assets for any new enrichment program.

The responsibility of creating and operating an extracurricular enrichment program can seem overwhelming. Looking at one component at a time may ease the stress level of the potential program director. The first question a program director should ask themselves is do you have the time necessary to dedicate to a program. There is no exact amount of time any program takes. Each program takes its own amount of time. A program that operates once a week inside the school in the teacher's classroom may require only minor commitment time and preparation. Larger more far-reaching programs will obviously require more time in preparation. Next, the consideration of the family of the program director must be addressed. If the program detracts from the value of their family time, something is sacrificed that will prove to be detrimental to the overall life of the program and the family of the program director. If it is possible to incorporate the family into the program, the time commitment may not be so detracting. The energy and enthusiasm required to create and steer a program must be acknowledged before embarking on the undertaking. The program director's health is a direct correlation to the health of the program. If surgery or some other medical condition is on the horizon, the program will suffer from the absence of the program director. My health and that of my aging mother were determining factors on whether I could continue my fully structured program. Maintaining the health of the program director is interconnected with the health of the program.

Selecting the correct amount and type of participants in the program is not as easy as posting or announcing it to the school. Some of the students that would be best served by such an enrichment program may be hesitant to become involved with the program because of a predisposition of failure and a feeling of being outside the school norm. Students from an underserved school population are prime candidates for the benefits of an enrichment program. Students that have been enriched throughout their school careers may find the program interesting but may have experiences that surpass the scope and vision of the program. Creating an optimum mix of highly skilled students and students that could benefit from skills provided by the program will contribute to the overall success of the enrichment activity.

Organizational skills and resource management must be considered by program directors as an integral part of the overall success of the activity. Acquiring these funds and resources may involve interactions with community members and school administration. A good working relationship with school administrators provides a valuable asset when it comes to resources and funding. These stakeholders play an important role in moving vision to reality. A program director very seldom goes it alone. The broader reaching the program, the more adult staff are necessary to operate the program. Staffing a program requires a different level of administration and interaction with adult mentors. Keeping in mind many of the adults that take part in an enrichment program may be volunteers, their time and skills are valuable, and they must always feel that their value is recognized. Keeping students and staff in good spirits and high morale is the responsibility of a program director and can never be neglected. Above all else, the extracurricular enrichment program involves the establishment of a learning community. Learning communities are living entities created by all participants and stakeholders. A program director must be able to manage the objective operations of the program and the subjective interactions between the participants. All these skills enable program directors to create and operate a successful extracurricular enrichment program.

7

The Fully Structured Program
(or the Whole Ball of Wax)

A fully structured program is the most comprehensive of all of the types of extracurricular enrichment programs presented. A fully structured program contains all aspects that must be considered throughout the life of the program. This type of program is the most time-consuming and energy-intensive to develop yet it contains the potential of being the most outstanding experience for all participants and staff. Done correctly, a fully structured program can provide the inclusion of an eclectic population that touches upon all demographics and provides opportunities for growth for each individual within the program structure. By examining each step taken to create a fully structured program, individuals and organizations can gain a better understanding of all the intricacies involved in bringing a life-changing opportunity to participants and staff.

My greatest program accomplishment was in the development of a fully structured program. This program existed independently from the school system yet benefited greatly from a collaboration with it and other stakeholders. An in-depth analysis of all of the steps taken to create this program and operate it will give a strong basis from the grassroots to the fully structured program. Fully structured programs provide the greatest opportunity for the enrichment of all participants. The demands

DOI: 10.4324/9781003254911-8

the development of such a program place upon a program director and other stakeholders enable the creation of an independent entity that brings a learning community to its highest levels. The successes of my fully structured program can be replicated by any person or organization willing to take the time and effort necessary to develop and implement the program. By understanding each step taken along the way of this program's development and implementation, individuals and organizations can successfully cut their own path through extracurricular enrichment program development.

The inability of a committee trying to develop a skills-based program is the starting point for the successful program development I was able to accomplish. There were many factors that needed to be elaborated on that helped facilitate this program's creation and successful implementation. I was in committee meetings sponsored by a school board director that had the goal of creating a program that would teach children skills. The committee chairman and other members of the committee were relying upon a documentary to spur the enthusiasm of the community and gain the involvement of stakeholders and participants. The idea behind the whole concept was meritorious. The inability to gain permission to show the video stalled the committee and left it adrift without direction and eventually the ideas and concepts faded into memory. The overarching concept the committee was trying to bring across was a skills-based curriculum presented to an inclusive body of participants.

The idea of providing skills-based experiences to students spurred my interest and enthusiasm. Seeing that the committee was going nowhere, I took it upon myself to create this dream program. The concept of the skills-based curriculum had been talked about throughout the community. A friend of mine, the chair of the economics department of the local college, had just finished a report on skills needed by local employers that were lacking in the current employee pool of the area. It was his report that started the development of an overall vision for what would become the Ben Franklin School of Industry. Ben Franklin was chosen as a model of a variety of successful skills and achievements. Basing the program on Ben Franklin's concepts and ideas were the fundamental building blocks necessary in the program's creation. The program was independent of the school district from where I worked but drew upon students from that district.

The needs of local businesses and employers were at the forefront of the skills that would be introduced and elaborated on by the staff. The educational concepts that would provide the framework for the program centered on constructivism and experiential learning. It was defined very clearly that the participants in the program would construct their knowledge from the experiences they took part in while participating in the program. With the assistance of my college professor friend, the overall vision of the program was developed. The program was skills-based and product- and goal-oriented. This simple yet inclusive vision statement was enough to stir the interests of the many stakeholders that took part in the pilot program initiative. My friend from the college proved to be my most valuable resource. His report was the driving force behind the enrichment initiative. His understanding of pilot programs also gave me a knowledge base that was more refined than my experiences with other extracurricular enrichment programs. His connection with the college brought the program into a collaboration with the college and facilitated the incorporation of college interns as part of the staff. The community in which the enrichment program serves is an important component in any program's success. My years of living within the community and interacting with a variety of organizations and individuals proved to be an asset that was necessary for the program to be a success.

My affiliation with local charitable organizations gave me a direct line to resources that those organizations possessed. The fact that the program was to serve local children motivated many of the members to vote positively when matters of finance and facilities were brought before the organizations. My membership provided a gateway to the use of an organization's building and grounds. Determining where a program can be held will impact the operational vision the program can provide. The facility we used had a large banquet hall with a library and several meeting rooms and workrooms available. This building was a crucial part of the overall success of the program. The grounds around the building were a semi-wetland environment. This environment was very enticing to several volunteers and staff. Once I had secured a location in which to house the program, determining how the program would be staffed was next on the agenda.

Having a positive relationship with my educational colleagues gave me a large pool of potential candidates for the staff. Since the overall vision involved a product and goal, I casually discussed the program with potential staff members. My discussions helped guide the choice of the final project the pilot program would initiate. The program would center around a team catapult building competition and a study of projectile motion. Other educational enrichment opportunities would also be included in the program to incorporate more of the skills Ben Franklin so amply demonstrated. Finding prospective teachers to help round out the roster of academic offerings was not difficult. There were plenty of my colleagues interested in the overall concepts of the program and how it would impact children's lives. A perfect fit of personalities and teaching styles of the staff would provide an already existing model of a learning community. By selecting the teachers from a group of friends, the bonds of cooperation and respect were already established. Each teacher brought more skills to be imparted to the students than the designated subject matter they taught in the classroom. All the staff collaborated to create an atmosphere of positive goal orientation.

My experience garnered from one of my mentor's fully structured programs introduced me to the concept of an intensive program. The Ben Franklin School of Industry was to run for one week, mimicking the school day but it was to be similar to an intensive college program. By intensive, I mean a nonstop immersion in learning and experiences that leaves no time for idleness or distraction. To create an intensive dynamic program, a well-mapped-out operational vision and a knowledge of smooth transformations from one activity to another are required. The selection of the subject matter to be presented during the one-week intensive program came about during a single meeting where all staff members were present. A spirit of collaboration permeated the meeting with each member adding more parts to the overall structure the program would assume. From that single meeting, a general curriculum was designed.

The programs would have a nutrition component as well as humanities and eco-science components. The main courses centering on catapult production would be industrial arts and physics. Rounding out each day's offering of academics would be the language arts and business communication sections. The physical education component would involve demonstrations and participation in different types of projectile motion. From throwing balls to an introduction to the bow and arrow, students would observe a demonstration and then take part in experiencing the concepts presented. All of the teaching staff were focused on the main goal of the program, which was the creation of a miniature version of a catapult that could propel a stuffed animal projectile 20 or 30 feet to strike a target. The students would be broken up into teams to compete in the competition that would have a definitive winner. Nutrition would be provided in the morning, at the midday break and a small snack before they departed the program for the day.

The nutrition component of the overall program was of equal importance as any other aspect of the program. Breakfast was served and a large banquet hall allowed for student groups to gather and the teachers to eat and interact with them. The impact of sharing a meal with your peers and your mentors created a stronger dynamic bond for the learning community. Lunchtime provided a perfect transition between activities and instruction. The end of the day snack eliminated the doldrums that occurred from a full day of activities and academics. The opportunities to interact with instructors during a meal create a more comfortable and casual atmosphere for interaction. Having someone on staff with restaurant experience (my wife) was crucial to the nutrition segment of the program. She had spent half of her working career in food service and was familiar with all aspects of preparing and serving meals. Her ability to prepare large banquet size meals proved invaluable for the overall success of the program. She was assisted by both students and interns from the college.

Both funding and food donations from local businesses provided the meals. Preparing meals and food for a large group of students requires an understanding of their special tastes and allergies. None of the student participants or instructors had any food allergies. This made food meal preparation more manageable. Learning about a food allergy as the food is being consumed could be very damaging to the student and the program. Comprehensive information about medical information, food and allergies is important. A number of students came from economically disadvantaged environments. Meals in the summer for these types of students may be very important in the lives of those students. An understanding of hunger issues among economically disadvantaged students should be something all teachers are aware of but most especially those that are operating an extracurricular activity. Hunger makes it hard to concentrate and learn. Knowing this simple fact put nutrition at the forefront and commencement of every session of the program. No food was wasted. Either food that was not eaten during a session was properly stored for the next day's meals or food that could not be stored was distributed to all of the students to take home to their families. The staff were well aware that some of the students were taking home the only meal their brothers and sisters would have that day. Students that we had recognized as nutrition deprived were given ample food at the end of every day to provide a meal for their families. The motivation of hunger for food may have been a greater driving force to bring the student to the program consistently than their hunger for academic knowledge.

The operational vision of the program started to take a more concrete structure as all components of the program began to mesh together. Once the generalized curriculum was agreed to by the teaching staff and the nutrition plan was developed, a cohesive operational vision was created. Knowing the final product like knowing the ending of the story allowed me as the director to create a step-by-step process to achieve our goal. Each class and activity helped to create a multidisciplinary learning community that integrated multiple levels of learning and learning styles. The sessions had diverse learning experiences each day. There was hands-on instruction and experimentation as well as lectures and discussions. Notetaking, reflection and other forms of language art communication were evident throughout the program. Working from a constructivist educational point of view, students and teachers were immersed in experiences that allowed them to construct their own knowledge and understanding of the information and activities. The program was based on experiential learning. Guiding the operational vision was the need for diverse learning experiences for each session. The element of surprise and unpredictable events kept the students' interest and motivated the instructors. Every day was different, yet every day consistently worked toward the product and goals of the overall program. Teachers moved from their comfort zone of their own subject area into other experiences that may have been new to them. The optimum goal of the learning community, in my humble opinion, is that everyone involved in the community is, in fact, a learner. When students see adults, they look upon them as mentors, learning new topics of lifelong learning that school and education try to stress. With the program's operational vision and overall vision well defined, the quest for funding and resources came to the forefront.

Funding and resources are a source of stress and anxiety for a program director. Early in my career, I visited a number of independently operated educational institutions. In meetings with the directors of every one of those institutions, funding was always on their minds. Talking with individuals that face the same challenges can often give a new direction to the topic. Each director that I spoke with had their own unique way of acquiring funds and resources yet all of them relied on the success and overall purpose of their programs. With students, specifically children, at the very heart of the program, stakeholders that can provide monetary support can more easily be approached.

Approaching an unfamiliar stakeholder and asking for money can be quite nerve-racking and sometimes frightening. It is at this point that a dedicated program director must take a deep breath, grit their teeth and face individuals with deep pockets and ask them to dig deep and provide some funding for a worthy cause. Fundraising and resources are so important that an entire chapter needs to be devoted to various techniques and methods to acquire the necessary monetary and material support a program requires. The operational and overall vision and the population the program will serve are the key components to acquiring a meeting with a monetary stakeholder and obtaining funding. Not all stakeholders will provide money. Some stakeholders have resources and materials they are able to provide. We were building catapults roughly the size of a grown human. A director wishing to create a product as a goal of the program must thoroughly understand the construction of the project. Before any funding or resources could be gathered for the program. a program director must know exactly what is needed for the program to operate. There can be unexpected expenditures of which a comprehensive budget will have taken into account.

The catapults were a topic I personally studied and was aware of similar projects done throughout the country. Diagrams and material lists were available, and I took full advantage, as well as discussed the construction of the catapults with the industrial arts teacher. My friendship with the head of the economics department of the local college allowed the printing of handbooks and brochures. Collaboration with the college opened the door for internships for their students. These student interns from the college were as valuable as any other member of staff. Their dedication, energy and youthfulness added a level of interaction with the student participants that could not have occurred without them. Monetary funding came from a variety of sources. Several of the sources were local employers who had been involved in the skills report of my collegiate friend. Wanting to have a stake in the overall community and access to potential employees provided the motivation for monetary donations. Because the program was just beginning and was operating independently from the school, nonprofit status was not granted, thus preventing any donation from being a tax deduction in that category. We were able to obtain an adequate amount of materials from local vendors including lumber, tools and food as well as funding from other local community sources. The handbook and brochures about the program were provided to the potential stakeholder.

Handbooks and brochures are not always necessary for fully structured programs. The handbook and brochures used by the Ben Franklin School of Industry were important components of the overall success of the program. I believe that all fully structured programs require some type of documentation that explains the purpose, mission and expectations of the program. My familiarity with programs of this sort allowed me to develop a handbook that was comprehensive yet easy to digest and understand by all participants, staff and stakeholders. In the handbook, the overall vision and operating vision were presented. Quotes from Ben Franklin were interspersed throughout the small eight-page handbook. Long-range goals were listed so that stakeholders could see beyond the one-week program. Various learning components were exemplified and a syllabus of the course offerings was included. Roles for staff and students as well as duties and behavior expectations were also part of the handbook. A trifold brochure was created and was used to advertise the program to potential student participants and stakeholders.

An application and a process of admission were designed for participants of the program. The application mimicked job applications, college applications and other documents. The program application was simpler and easier to understand and provided a beginning for students to experience the application process. The program was advertised throughout the school, most especially within my classroom. A target size of 20 students was the initial goal for the program. With 20 students, a ratio of one adult to five students would be possible. In the end, the program served 17 students. Having a weeklong summer camp that was academically oriented was not a traditional program that might interest students during their school vacation time. A select group of students came from active parents that were either teachers or business owners that were aware of the program from its inception. All other students needed to be recruited in various ways. The application process and interview process that admission to the program required frightened some students from attempting to participate. The students had repeatedly experienced rejection and felt that the application and interview process was just another way for them to be told they did not measure up. Trusting in me to not let them down they bravely filled out the applications and went through the interview process. The interview and application were included in the overall enrichment program agenda because they gave real-world experience to the students. Every student that applied and went through the interview process was accepted and they received an acceptance letter that was given out at school. Seeing their eyes light up when they read something that said that they were worthy and made the cut (though there was no cut) is a memory I will cherish forever. For many of them, this was the first time they were accepted into something that they wanted to do. Before the program even began, it was making a difference in the lives of the participants. The mix of students included the gifted and talented, the quiet and often unnoticed hard-working students and students with special needs. Economically, the group covered the gambit from the most economically challenged to the most affluent. This mix of students created an extraordinary learning community and stood as a glowing example of how given a common goal and common experiences diverse groups can pull together and become a positive energized community.

The program started with an exciting opening ceremony and never lost momentum through the five days it occurred. The students were so enthusiastic that a very rare attendance situation occurred. The program saw 100% attendance throughout the entire length of the program. Some of the students that participated had attendance issues in the traditional school but this program motivated them to overcome their resistance to education and become part of a greater community. Though I do not know if any lasting friendships were established. For one brief moment in time, friendship, cooperation, teamwork and acceptance prevailed. The program was so successful the student participants, as well as the staff, demanded that it continue throughout the coming school year and through the following summers.

The program ran for four consecutive years and provided afterschool and summer enrichment for many participants. As a four-year pilot program with continuing success, we hoped to expand and continue it. Unfortunately, health concerns and family matters demanded that we retire the program. It is the writing of this book that allows me to continue the success of the Ben Franklin school of industry and hopefully pass it on to other energetic and dedicated program directors. It was my decision to retire the program. Its successful existence allows me the opportunity to share the knowledge and experience I acquired during its operation.

From the experiences at the Ben Franklin School of Industry, a step-by-step process to create a fully structured program can be presented. The overarching concepts that enable a program director and their team to create this enrichment activity are the foundation that I recommend for all future fully structured programs. Based on both community and student needs for skills that transfer directly to the workforce and experiences that are not normally available in a standard school day made the program so valuable. The needs of the stakeholders that supported the program and the students that participated in it coincided. With this type of foundation, extracurricular enrichment fully structured programs can be developed.

Utilizing existing needs and an overall vision that stirs the interest of participants and stakeholders alike can be created. The competition component and the construction product were guiding factors that made the operation vision tangible and real. The availability of print media to convey concepts and ideas about the prospective program enabled participants and stakeholders to grasp the far-reaching yet obtainable goals of the week-long enrichment activities. Preparing for the one-week program required three months of preliminary work. As program director, I had to develop the concepts and curriculum that would be presented and put them into an easily understandable form. My experience in the advertising field allowed me to create the necessary print material that conveyed the program's intent in the most positive light. By handing potential funding sources, material that was in a well-developed and refined manner differentiated the program from other charitable endeavors. Most of the time, people come to funding sources with merely an idea or a program presented with a single sheet of paper with the time, place and type of activity described. It then becomes one more charitable event asking for funding from businesses. This enrichment program with its collaboration with the local college and support from a business organization allowed more avenues for funding to be available. The community organization that I belong to also provided funding as well as the location to hold the weeklong event. The application and interview process were discussed and refined by members of the staff. Recruitment and information about the existence of the program were provided a month in advance to the prospective student participants. Even three months before the program's start, time was of the essence. Finalization of the overall operation of the program did not occur until the night before the program was to begin.

The staff and interns met for a brief time the day before the start date of the program. The college provided three student interns. These interns were a major factor in the program's success. Not only did they interact positively with the students, but they took upon themselves responsibilities above and beyond their initial duties. They became immersed in the overall experience and their enthusiasm mixed with the enthusiasm of the teachers and students created a weeklong festival-type atmosphere where smiles and laughter abounded. It behooves prospective program directors and administrators to make sure their contacts with higher education institutions are utilized. I was lucky to have a good friend that was not only responsible for the report that motivated the program's inception but was also willing to connect me with the appropriate individuals at the college so interns could be acquired.

Firm grounding in reality and collaboration with other organizations increase the potential success of any extracurricular program. Community connections provide more sources of potential stakeholders and funding. Belonging to a service organization proved to be very advantageous and is highly recommended for potential program directors, administrators and other staff. Service organizations may not have the funding necessary to assist in the program but may provide a direction for program directors to find resources and funding. The more a program can tie the students' needs to the community's needs, the more chance of gathering effective stakeholders. The development of a daily operational agenda is another component that must be present before contacting stakeholders and implementing the program. Students do not need to know what events will occur each day during the life of the program but staff and stakeholders need to have that information available. Stakeholders only need a vague idea of what will happen day by day but staff need a well-defined agenda as well as specific job assignments. Vague and ambiguous positions will lead to confusion and dilute the overall success of the program and its goals and products.

Keeping the goal of the program at the forefront of the thoughts of the administrators and staff will prevent events from distracting staff and participants. Clarity of purpose cannot be overstated. Casual reflective discussions at the end of each session with staff members added more strength to the direction of the program. Reflective thought after every program session was built into the program director's duties. Objective reflective thought provided me with a way to refine each session as the program progressed and developed a smooth-running operation. Students reflected on their experiences every day during the language arts component of the program. They used these reflections to compose thank-you letters sent out to all stakeholders of the program. Daily interaction with students allowed each teacher and staff member to meet individual needs and the group purpose more readily.

The competition aspect of the program did not create an adversarial position between the student groups. The opposite occurred. Groups that had found success at some aspect of the construction of the catapult readily shared their success with the other teams. With just minor directed interaction, mealtime furthered the students' cooperative atmosphere and exchange of ideas. From reflection to discussion, conversations were rich with individual development and growth. The enrichment process that the program had hoped to achieve far exceeded expectations by emphasizing what each member thought and allowing them to verbalize it. The Ben Franklin School of Industry was originally planned to be a one-week intensive enrichment program taking place a week after school ended for the summer. The overwhelming success of the one-week program and the demands of the participants and the staff transformed the weeklong program into a continuous extracurricular enrichment program that ran for a total of four consecutive years.

The initial population of participants consisted of mostly high school students grades nine through 12 but also included my daughter and two other middle school students. As the program became more refined, it served students from ages ten through 20. The academic offerings and life skills instruction included resumes and acquiring driver licenses. With its connection and collaboration with the local college, diverse cultures and religions were included in the program. The staff and volunteers changed from time to time but the program director remained consistent throughout the length of the project. Students that graduated from high school returned to the program to act as interns and assist in any way they could. The overall and operational goals remained directly guided by the overall and operational visions. The strong initial structure of the program allowed for growth and development while still maintaining its integrity and original purpose. Fully structured programs can evolve while still staying true to their initial development.

Looking at the start to finish process of this fully structured program will enable future program directors, administration and other stakeholders the ability to develop their own fully structured extracurricular enrichment program. Before the program even began, a three-month period of development was necessary. During this time, the overall vision was refined and the operational vision was constructed. The necessary print materials helped to solidify the program's overall direction and purpose. These written documents gave a concrete foundation for stakeholders to support as well as to garner staff and student participants. In developing the print materials, the program and its goals could be clarified and maintained. Putting down on paper the ideas and concepts that a program director wishes to instill in the operation of the program provides a clarity of purpose for anyone to see. The curriculum changed with each new set of sessions. The original catapult construction and projectile motion goal was utilized only for the weeklong summer program. Hydroponics, alternative energy sources and ecological studies were just some of the future offerings the program presented as it grew.

During the school year, the program operated one day a week, beginning as the school day concluded and ending three hours later. The one day a week program saw a variety of participants and attendance varied from 15 to 25 students. The summer week-long program saw an increase from the initial 17 students served to 20 to 25 students depending on the year. The goals and products of each separate session group changed but the concept of goals and products never changed. The integrity of the original program and structure was always the framework that each new session set would rely upon.

The selection process for student participants continued to require a refined application and often students provided references from other teachers and administrators and alumni of the program. The broad outreach necessary to create the original program continued and allowed for a diverse student population with significant representation from traditionally underrepresented demographics. The enthusiasm of the students and the appreciation of the time mentors spent with them were evident throughout the existence of the program. The strong feeling of accomplishment permeated every operation session and each year. The college continued its collaboration by providing interns and the availability of their printing department and faculty.

Funding the program required continuous effort. Stakeholders that had originally funded the pilot program were not always able to continue their support. New sources of revenue and fundraising tactics always had to be developed. Some paid staff had to take reduced wages or merely volunteer their time in order to keep the program operating. The demands of fundraising work were constant stresses on the program director. Similar to program directors from other operations, the finding of money and sources of revenue were constantly at the forefront of the program director. The biggest issue by far was maintaining a steady revenue stream. The initial seed money provided by my association with the community service group dried up and forced me to find alternative sources of funding. Though funding was a problem, it was not the reason the program ended.

The health demands upon a program director cannot be overstated. It is highly recommended that a very solid support group bolster the program director and the program. Trying to do all things for all people will eventually lead to burnout for a program director. The location and all of the resources of the facility provided remained consistent throughout the life of the program. Though the monetary support from the service organization dwindled, the building and all of the utilities and insurance necessary to operate a program were still provided. Having a place to hold an enrichment activity is as important as the activity itself. Without a building that had a kitchen, banquet hall, large classroom area and library, the program would not have succeeded to the level that it did. It can be stated clearly that regardless of how grand the idea is, without the brick-and-mortar place to conduct the activity, there can be no activity.

The choice of activities for each session of the program was drawn from student interest as well as community interest and need. With each new offering, a clear understanding of the skills that would be presented and acquired by the students was developed. The industrial arts component was always present throughout the life of the program. Hands-on experience with every activity differentiated the program's enrichment of its students from other academic enrichment programs. When constructing an enrichment program, multiple learning styles and entry points should be considered. The more diverse the experiences the student participants have, the greater the enrichment impact will be on them. Continuing to base the program's educational theory on constructivism and experiential learning insured that the integrity of the initial overall vision was maintained. Basics of the operational vision were always present.

As seen throughout this book, the stressing of attendance and knowing where each individual participant is at any given time is as crucial to the operation of the program as it is to the operation of a classroom or school. Clearly defining the individual roles of students, mentors and other volunteers eliminates ambiguity and prevents the program from degenerating into just a group of people gathering together. The fluid transition from one activity to another always encouraged engagement in the new activity. Meals provided at the beginning of the after-school program gave a welcome break from the school day to the activities of the enrichment program. This brief yet very important component was never absent throughout all sets of program sessions. Reflections and rewards for achievements, taking home the products the students created and competing in competitions made every session worthwhile. Community connections helped broaden the students' appreciation for their own community and how to interact with the community. At the end of each program session, a celebration of achievement and accomplishment was held. Stakeholders, staff and students, as well as their parents, were invited to participate in the celebration. The students' accomplishments and products were exhibited and all present could see the overall impact the program had on the participants. A truly successful extracurricular enrichment program will positively transform all that take part in the program.

8

Fear of Funding (or Beggars Can't Be Choosers)

Every program director that I have ever met has been in a constant search for funding to maintain their program. Funding comes from a variety of sources and no one source can be depended on to constantly fund a program. How to acquire funding and where to look for funding are important skills that program directors must possess or someone within the staff must possess. A program director must take the funding of the program on entirely. This never-ending search for funding is exhausting. It may well be the reason that many programs, regardless of their successes, terminate. I struggled with funding throughout my entire career in creating extracurricular enrichment programs. There are some key points that can help in the search for funding or the creation of revenue sources. Sometimes, the program director will have to dig into their own finances to support the program they created. The program director will be the last one to get monetary remuneration for their efforts. Unlike a business where the boss pays themselves first then everyone else gets what's leftover, the enrichment program often leaves the program director with the lowest of salaries. Well-established programs that have support and budgets from school districts or organizations will find the funding issue less demanding. Even programs under the budget umbrella of the school district need to raise money for

DOI: 10.4324/9781003254911-9

special events and purposes. Sometimes, finding funding can be as simple as filling out a budget form but other times it can be complex and multifaceted. The more avenues a program director has available to find funding, the higher the probability of fully funding the program will occur.

Ideally, being part of a school district's budget eases the monetary tensions and pressures of the program director. If the program is new, presenting the ideas and concepts to the district curriculum director can often assist in the search for financial support. The curriculum director of the school district is well aware of many different programs from the state and federal government that support extracurricular activities. The more inclusive these activities are, the more likely the program will fit into some sort of government program. The overall vision and operating vision of the program are the first things a program director should be able to present to prospective stakeholders. The first starting point for acquiring the necessary financial means to operate the program should start at the organization that is directly connected to the student population the program will serve. If the school administration approaches a prospective program director, the budget for the program is most likely already in place. Working with an organization such as the school district can provide the brick-and-mortar location that is also crucial to the operation of any program. Having a place to hold a program must be counted into the overall operating costs of the program itself. Renting or purchasing a place to house an extracurricular enrichment program is not something a new program director should consider. All my successful programs had a free-of-charge location in which to hold the activities.

One overlooked expense is insurance liability. Any program that involves children is going to have liability. Insurance for the participants' safety and covering any accidents that could occur often goes unnoticed by program directors working within an organization. If the program is freestanding and unaffiliated with any larger organization, the purchasing of insurance must be done and it comes at a great expense. If it had not been for the organizations' insurances that my program was attached to, many of the most successful of my programs would never have come into existence. Buildings that house programs must have insurance. Organizations that host programs must have insurance. The larger the organization, such as a school district, the greater the umbrella of its insurance policies, and thus, protection for the program staff and participants. Being part of a larger organization or school district may not provide the program with direct financial support but by providing the insurance and utilities a large financial burden can be eased. Stakeholders can be funding sources and resource contributors in various forms. Some stakeholders can provide monetary funds, others can provide needed materials and others can provide knowledge and time.

The easiest place to get funding can be found by looking in the mirror. If your vision for an extracurricular enrichment program is so strong, be prepared to support it financially. For the grassroots and the semi-structured program, most materials and money can come directly from your purse or wallet. If you are willing to freely give of your time, that in and of itself is a donation. Depending on the size of the student group that you'll be enriching, a modest budget may suffice. The program director may have to provide snacks and other materials. Some of the materials may already be present in the classroom. Other materials can be gathered from associates and colleagues in the school. By sharing the goings-on of your program with your colleagues, you may find that some of them want to contribute to the children and the success of the program. It is not unheard of for a home economics teacher to provide snacks and food that was cooked by students in their classroom. Some colleagues may have resources sitting idle in their room that they no longer want. Scavenging the school for materials can supply some surprising treasures.

Depending on the type of program, students may have some of the necessary materials themselves. For instance, take a collectible card game. Students that want to be part of a larger group playing this card game may have the necessary card decks and other materials to play the game. If the students have all the necessary resources and materials for the program to operate, all the program director needs to do is find a location. A classroom after school hours is almost always available. Without very much difficulty, a classroom teacher can avail their classroom to a variety of activities. Students may also be willing to provide their own snacks, but snacks should be available for those students that forget or cannot afford to purchase them. As a rule of thumb, the current tax deduction for teaching materials can be used as a guideline for how much money a program director can invest in the project. Asking students to contribute to the funding of the project can lead to a lot of complexities. Managing other people's money, most especially students, is not something I would ever recommend, and I avoided it throughout my entire career. Money will always be an issue, and the more control of the sources of funding the program director has, the more responsibility to keep accurate records will be demanded.

A careful accounting and documenting of all funds and materials purchased for the program must occur. Inconsistent accounting can lead to uncomfortable accusations and may jeopardize the entire program. The larger the funding, the more judicious the handling of that funding must be. Most student organizations have an established method of accounting and fund allocation. These organizations have guidelines and bylaws that must be adhered to in order to continue operation. If an enrichment program wishes to be part of a larger organizational group, then another level of structure will have to be added.

Establishing a deeper connection with the school should wait until the program has reached maturity and proven that it has longevity. Usually, bank accounts are set up by an administrative officer. The grassroots and semi-structured programs may only be in existence for a few years. Therefore, taking on a larger structure and the burden of the operations of a club within a school district may not be advantageous to the success of the program. Once the enrichment program starts, outside revenue sources may appear. Donations from outside sources often occur. The outside sources might be the parents themselves, community organizations or businesses. Whatever the source, careful accounting and transparency must be in place. Paper trails provide ample proof of the allocation of funds. If a program director and program exist outside of an organizational structure, other components must be put in place.

The fully structured program that I created existed outside of the jurisdiction of the school. It was housed in another facility owned by a community organization. Initially, all funding and invoices were turned over to the organization's secretary and treasurer. All checks to vendors and staff were endorsed by the president of the organization. A full reporting of revenue and expenditures was required to operate the program within the facility. Later, the program got its own bank account, accountant and lawyer. All expenditures required the approval of the Board of Directors that had been established for the program and all revenue was reported. Money is crucial and it has often been mismanaged by individuals.

Mismanaging funds can destroy any good that a program accomplished. Programs that have well-documented accounting are more likely to receive a nonprofit designation by the government. This nonprofit designation assists in all levels of fundraising. Acquiring such a nonprofit status is not easy. Both my mentors took years to get their programs to nonprofit status and both required the assistance of professional legal services. It is not uncommon for individuals within an organization that is being petitioned for funding to recommend a nonprofit status. They may have had experience in their prior organizations that had the nonprofit status. Grants and other donations most likely require a program to already have nonprofit status. Individuals that suggest applying for grants may not know the full process to acquire nonprofit status. It should also be noted that grants often come with stipulations that must be strictly followed. The more strings that get attached to funding, the more difficult the navigation through the creative process of bringing an enrichment program to life will be. The most common method of acquiring funds for a new program is meeting with the leadership of businesses or organizations.

Business owners regularly are asked to donate to worthy causes around their community. Depending on the time of year, two to three organizations can stop by a business to ask for a donation. These owners only have a limited amount of charitable funds they can give. If they had unlimited resources, they would most likely donate to all causes that ask for funding. The reality of the situation is some funding relies strictly on timing. If you are the first to ask for funding for your program that business quarter, you may well receive it. If you're the third person in one day to come in and ask for a donation, you may not get a very cordial greeting or the funding that you desire. The personal connections the program director has with their community and businesses are a plus when it comes to funding requests. Long-standing friendships with individuals that are dedicated to their community whether it is as business leaders or as organizational leaders can prove one of the best sources to finance a worthy program.

The Ben Franklin School of Industry received its largest single donation from the service organization that I had belonged to for over 25 years. A member had left an endowment of $15,000 to the organization as long as it was spent on charitable projects. I presented the Ben Franklin School of Industry's overall vision and operating vision as well as brochures to all of the members at the meeting that would decide the amount of funding the program would receive. The meeting was tense. Some members did not want to allocate the amount of money that I needed to operate the program and several hours of debate took place. In the end, $3000 was donated as seed money to start the program as well as to the facility, utilities and other resources. This single source of funding set the stage for the program to begin.

The next step in the process of gaining funding was to set up meetings with various business leaders throughout the community. The program was based on a skills report that was completed for the area business leaders. The program was designed to meet the needs of employment that were identified within the report. The businesses that had taken part in the study all contributed to the initial program's starting fund. My funding drive began in early spring. It should be noted that most charitable organizations, banks and other places that donate often set their donation schedule in late December and early January. Timing is very important. When I went to the local banks for funding, they thought the cause was worthy, but unfortunately, they had allocated all their funds to other charities that January. Obtaining funding for an ongoing enrichment program will be a full-time process. There are certain methods I can recommend that have worked to obtain donations and/or resources.

For several different programs, local businesses did not donate money but rather materials. Materials used for the products and goals of the program are just as valuable as monetary resources. Depending on the project, a creative program director may be able to gain materials such as paint or lumber. Even, tools can be acquired from businesses such as hardware stores. Prizes needed for competitions can come from a variety of places. If a business has been petitioned time and time again by other charities, clearing out their stock room of some unneeded merchandise can work as prizes and incentives for the student participants. The concept of only money being the type of donation a program needs should be dropped and thinking outside the box replace it. Making a list of all the materials and tools needed to create the product of the program enables a program director to look beyond money as the only way a program can operate.

In discussing the program with potential stakeholders, some type of documentation, brochure, poster or other visual aid will be advantageous to your cause. Being open to all varieties of assistance to accomplish your overall goals increases the probability of success of the program. One stakeholder of my fully structured program was unwilling to donate money but was having a garage sale and allowed me to take whatever tools and other materials for free. Having your information in hand and seeing a garage sale in your neighborhood may prove beneficial if there are items and materials that the host of the garage sale may willingly donate. If you do not ask, you may not receive. Getting past the initial fear of asking for donations or a contribution or materials is something a program director must do. Materials and resources as well as money are not the only things that can be donated to make a program successful.

When I petitioned a local entrepreneur in environmental sciences for assistance with the program, I did not expect him to volunteer his expertise on a regular basis as a mentor. The value of the contribution of this expertise in environmental science was immeasurable. Though he was not willing to donate money, his time and knowledge could not be replaced. As he became increasingly involved with the students of the program, he used his own money to purchase science kits and other learning material for the program. Other assistance can be gathered from businesses such as discount transportation costs. A field trip to a science center was made possible by a bus company willing to provide services at cost and no profit. Other transportation for programs can be arranged at discount prices from local public transportation companies. Creative thinking and a willingness to accept any type of contribution will give a program a greater connection with stakeholders and build a positive atmosphere in the community for the program.

The students that participate in the program can be a great asset when acquiring donations. Any opportunity to involve the participants in the enrichment program with the community should be considered. As I went from one business to another asking for financial aid for the program, I was accompanied by several of the students that benefited from the program. Their input in the process and presence when asking for donations brings even more reality to the concept of the program. It is much harder for business owners to refuse those that would benefit from their contribution when they are looking them in the eye. Students lend their experience in participating in the program as a testimony to the program's success. Seeing the impact, a monetary donation can have on the lives of the student participants allows the business owner a personal connection with the beneficiaries. Concluding projects and performances with invitations to all stakeholders and prospective stakeholders are extremely helpful in garnering more support throughout the community. Any chance to reach a larger audience with the knowledge of what the program does and hopes to accomplish should be pursued.

Newspaper articles and radio shows assist in gaining new stakeholders and justifying the continuation of support from existing stakeholders. The local public broadcasting station did an entire community program in which the Ben Franklin School of Industry was one of the features. This broadcast brought more community knowledge to the existence of the program and helped in acquiring new stakeholders. To maintain contributions from existing stakeholders, some type of demonstration of gratitude is important. Handwritten thank-you letters are just one very important aspect of helping in continuing financial support from stakeholders. Press releases, photographs and other documentation that supports the program should be provided to every stakeholder and future stakeholder. If students can create a product such as a sign for the business, such a gift is often very well received. There are other ways the participants in the program can help to raise funds. These methods are often your typical fundraising techniques.

Student-driven fundraisers are a mainstay of clubs and organizations from within and outside the school. Candy sales are some of your more typical methods to raise funds. Pizza sales and some food sales also fit into this category. There are companies devoted to fundraising and have everything from cookie dough to candles for students to go door to door and sell. The management of these fundraisers is always stressful and time-consuming. Even the most seasoned fundraising individual realizes gathering the funds, distributing the orders and making sure every customer is satisfied is not to be taken lightly. Depending on what the funds will be used for will dictate how large the fundraising activity will need to be. Selling subs for instance can raise a few hundred dollars but that is hardly enough to finance an entire program. The sub-sale that my students conducted was to raise enough money to pay for admission into a science center. A local utility company donated a substantial amount that allowed us to acquire the services from the local school bus company. The school bus company provided a discount for their vehicle and services. With the help of a number of volunteers, the distribution of the subs went smoothly. If a program director has never run a student-driven fundraiser, consulting a colleague that is familiar with the ins and outs of such fundraising is advised.

For instance, take candy sales. One must know where the candy can initially be acquired and how much profit can be made by the sale of each box of candy. Knowing the amount of money necessary to be raised allows the program director to allocate the fundraising material to each student. Some students will sell more than their share while others will sell less. Running on a tight budget where every sale counts, might make your financial goal difficult to achieve. Like all things, anything that can go wrong most likely will go wrong. Nothing can be more frustrating than mixed-up orders, lost orders or incomplete orders. All these things can and have occurred when involved in selling items. Asking students to contribute from their own funds or their parents' funds for an outing or a special event is possible but not recommended. If your program is quite inclusive there will be a number of economically disadvantaged students that will be unable to meet the financial demands and obligations this type of fundraising requires.

A tried-and-true method of fundraising used by organizations throughout the country is the rummage sale. Like a garage sale, items that are no longer of any use to an individual family can be donated. This enables all students and their families to participate. Going to local merchants and asking for donations for this type of sale can also be possible. There are other creative ways funds can be obtained for your program by utilizing the skills of the students and volunteers.

The facility that the Ben Franklin School of Industry utilized had a large kitchen and banquet hall. The service organization had several large gatherings and rather than have them catered by an outside vendor, the organizations chose to utilize the students and staff of the Ben Franklin school. This type of food service fundraising can gather a large amount of money very quickly but requires skilled staff to train and manage the operation of food service. If a program does not have a staff member with food service experience, reaching out to colleagues and staff of the school or organization may provide the individual that can assist in the success of this endeavor. Hosting banquets provides a venue where the students in the program can be accentuated. By providing a great atmosphere and a delicious meal, more stakeholders can be acquired. Food service experience provides another skill for the student participants of the program.

Though it may not have been the main objective of the program, preparing and serving food as well as cleanup are valuable skills that can be utilized in future employment by the students. The team-building experience of working to create an event and hosting it brings the student participants closer to each other and strengthens the overall learning community the program should be establishing. Another method of gathering funds utilizes the student's time and energy in assisting other larger organizations in their venues. A local utility company hosted a gathering for all of its customers once a year. Students from the Ben Franklin school provided the cleanup crew and the delivery service for the organization's event. The organization donated money consummate to the number of student participants and the hours they worked. Membership in community organizations and businesses is not necessary to have the program's participants selected to provide their time in service. Knowledge of the community and its organizations is important and should be cultivated at every opportunity. Successful programs are always on the lookout for potential donors and methods to raise money.

The more involved students of the program are with their community, the more opportunities for acquiring new stakeholders and funding arise. Connections with colleges and universities in the area are almost always positive influences on the program. Though a new program may lack the nonprofit status and the established narrative to acquire grant money, collaboration and affiliation with larger organizations that do get grants can lead to support and funding. A local college may be given a grant to revitalize the local community. Knowledge of the grant and the individuals that are overseeing the funding allocations can be helpful. The more community connected your program is, the more likely it is to garner support from organizations that have been granted money to assist the community. Helping young community members take part in revitalizing their own neighborhood is a worthy cause and lends itself to financial support from grant recipients. Knowledge of what is going on around the school in which the students that participate in the program are connected to cannot be overstated. Existing in a vacuum does not lend itself to community connections and the funds that are possible from those connections. The unique skills of the student participants can sometimes create opportunities to acquire funding and resources by the sharing of those skills.

One program that I operated involved computer languages and the construction of web pages. To move the program forward, the acquisition of a high-end computer was necessary. By speaking with the curriculum director of the school district the program was attached to, a unique but not unheard of means of acquiring the computer occurred. The curriculum director of the school district saw an opportunity to provide a teacher in-service program and connected it to a grant that allowed for technology acquisition. The students involved in this enrichment program had the knowledge of computers and webpage design that they were willing to share with teachers of the district and provide an in-service program for them. Teachers came for a week in the summer to be instructed on how to build and maintain web pages for their classrooms. A variety of skills were taught to the teachers to create their own web pages or the work was done by the students to create their web pages for the teachers' classrooms. The program was touted throughout the district and the area as a method to put students in as instructors and teachers as learners. The skills the students acquired from being the instructors of the program allowed them to add a significant section to their curriculum vitae. The pride the students took from being the driving force behind the acquisition of their dream computer encouraged them to push the limits of their skills even further.

The students' association with the teachers in the district and the technology department facilitated the permissions necessary for them to create their greatest project. With the blessings of the superintendent and the curriculum director, for one day at the end of their senior year, through networking all the computers in the district, they created a supercomputer that allowed them to render a complex 3D picture in record time. This achievement was included in their applications to colleges and future employment. Proving that extraordinary extracurricular enrichment programs create extraordinary opportunities for their participants.

Fundraising will always be the 800-pound gorilla in the room. It would be wonderful if all the funds necessary to operate the activities of every program director's dreams were available.

In reality, funding usually falls short or just barely meets the threshold needed to continue the activity. A program director alone may experience burnout if they are wearing too many hats to get their program going. The fundraising component is grueling and can never be overstated in its importance. Having more than one person spearheading fundraising opportunities is much more likely to prevent burnout from those in charge of the program. Acquiring the nonprofit status that allows for grants and directly tax-deductible donations from stakeholders takes time. A narrative of exactly how the program began and operates is required for this type of designation. Gaining nonprofit status often requires legal assistance and discussion with other experts that have already traveled that path. Once the nonprofit status is acquired, programs can accelerate their scope and depth as well as increase the population of student participants.

Connecting the program to establish nonprofits such as school districts and churches and other community organizations can ease the physical and mental challenges placed upon the fundraisers. The more open to new methods of fundraising a program director is, the more likely new ways to raise money will appear. Establishing connections throughout the community and businesses is almost an essential part of any successful extracurricular enrichment program. Keeping your light under a basket will not help in the generation of revenue to operate the program.

Public relations and communication with the school's community create opportunities for future stakeholder involvement. Any type of newspaper article or press release will have a positive impact on the program. The more local recognition the program can acquire will directly impact future stakeholder interest. A connection with the local newspaper is more a necessity than a luxury. My involvement with the community put me in touch with the editors of the local newspaper. I utilized that connection each time something worthy of print occurred or would occur in the program. Front page articles in small-town newspapers bring importance and significance to extracurricular enrichment programs and their activities. Good news is important in local newspapers. Communities love to read about their youth doing well.

At every opportunity let the community know what you are doing. Spread the word, talk to people, do whatever it takes to gain the positive recognition the program deserves. Serving young people in the community is close to the hearts of many community members. Keep that in mind, your strongest fundraisers are the students. They do not need to be the strongest sellers of candy and other items. They need to prosper and have a brighter future because of their participation in the program. Volunteering as a group to community-based efforts also gains recognition for the program and its participants. Informing local government officials and state government officials can have surprising benefits.

Most state senators and representatives peruse the local newspapers for articles about their citizens. These representatives and senators are involved in a variety of charitable activities. The state senator connected to the district that housed the Ben Franklin school donated half a prize-winning hog that she purchased at the county fair auction. That food donation fed students for several weeks of the program. The value of nonmonetary donations can be just as important as monetary donations. Resources, materials and services can have a significant impact on the success of a program. The collaboration with the local college provided the print media that advertised and supported the fully structured program I created. By deferring the cost of printing, more funding could be allocated to other parts of the program. Expert volunteers add an unmeasurable value to the operation of the program. The time a community member donates to instruct students may have a value that far surpasses the overall operating budget of the program. The acquisition funding, services, resources, materials and whatnot still center on a clearly defined overall vision for the program and a soundly structured operational vision. The more the program director knows about the program and its goals, and can convey them articulately to stakeholders, the higher the chance of the program gaining support.

The Conclusion (or the Show Has Just Begun)

One of the most rewarding experiences an educator can have is helping a student achieve a goal beyond the student's expectations. Taking part as a student acquires a new and valuable skill is equally rewarding. Helping a student refine their fundamentals to a level of mastery can bring an educator great satisfaction. These events in a student's life can be peak experiences and are often facilitated by an enrichment experience. The extracurricular enrichment program concept helps students go beyond their expectations and perceived limitations. The enrichment program presents opportunities for students to achieve goals they never thought possible or for creating a product that they believed was beyond their abilities. The enrichment programs presented in this book are one method that allows students to experience the satisfaction and surprise of high-end performance. An educator must believe that all students can achieve beyond the levels and limitations their mind has set for themselves. Enrichment programs when properly executed bring out the best in a student. The standard school day provides an opportunity for students to gain fundamental knowledge necessary to be utilized in higher-performing tasks.

Without the fundamentals, there can be very little enrichment that will be effective and long-lasting. The normal school day is filled with opportunities to gain fundamental skills and knowledge. It is often difficult for educators to provide enrichment programs within the confines of the eight-hour school day. The extracurricular program allows educators, schools and other organizations dedicated to student achievement to present opportunities for students to go beyond the fundamental level of learning. This is not to say that an enrichment program cannot present new fundamentals that may have been alien to a student's skill set before the enrichment program. New skills and

DOI: 10.4324/9781003254911-10

fundamentals are also enriching for students. The enrichment programs that educators and schools present should not follow the same formats found in the standard classroom. Enrichment programs need to differentiate themselves from standard school classroom practices and elevate the level of learning presented to the students. When an educator or school district seeks to create an extracurricular enrichment program, the initial consideration must be the students. The whole purpose of the enrichment program is to bring students to new levels of achievement. Without the students, there can be no program. Without the students, there really can't be a school. Students are the reason for the activities in standard school days and in extracurricular enrichment programs.

What type of student benefits most from enrichment programs? All students benefit from enrichment programs. Every student is able to participate in an enrichment program. Not all enrichment programs are for all students but all students can take part in various programs. Some enrichment programs are specifically designed for a student with a specific interest such as computer programming. Not every student in the school wants to be a computer programmer so an enrichment program designed for programming will not be something that interests all students. Ideally, there should be enough enrichment programs available so that a student can find an enrichment program that coincides with their interests. Extracurricular enrichment program design can target a specific interest type or can be diverse enough that all students can find something of interest in the program. Some programs are specifically geared toward an interest while others are enriching by their very nature. Programs that deal with art and writing may not appeal to students with mechanical interests.

A program that has a diverse set of topics or a single topic that can be diverse in its presentation and application can draw upon a large student population. Team competitions that have a number of components and skill requirements can introduce students to new experiences and also give them a chance to excel at their personal interests. An enrichment program that is multidisciplinary allows students a chance to experience disciplines outside their comfort zone but also work with familiar disciplines. This type of enrichment program brings students to a higher level of achievement in their major interests and allows them an entry point to a new educational topic. The type of program structure will dictate the type of students that are best suited for the enrichment program.

The four types of programs discussed in this book can be geared to fit any student group's interests. Some are more conducive to diverse groups while others are more effective with specifically targeted groups. The number of students that an enrichment program can have as participants depends on the level of individual attention required by a facilitator or program director. A ratio of one instructor for every five to seven students provides adequate instruction time for each individual. Larger groups can be accommodated depending on the subject matter, goals and products. In a mathematics camp that I held in the summer, 12 to 15 students could successfully participate and receive an enriching experience. Mural painting was another enrichment program I created. Groups of two to four students working on any one section of the mural proved to be the most effective. In this type of program, there were other activities available so students could circulate between activities and receive the necessary adult attention to create an enriching experience. A large fully structured program that has a number of facilitators can accommodate a larger number of student participants. Keeping in mind the same ratio of instructor to students, which allows for ample individual instruction, will dictate the number of adult facilitators necessary for the program to operate effectively.

If there are five instructors, the program can accommodate 25 students or even up to 35 students. As long as the program director keeps in mind the need for individualized instructions in order to facilitate a truly enriching program, a correct balance of students to instructors will be maintained. An enrichment program may sometimes be constrained by the space and resources available. If there are only enough construction materials to build ten birdhouses, then the program can only accommodate ten students. If the space available is small, the number of students must be small. A word of warning, just because a space can accommodate 100 students that does not mean 100 students should be the population of participants.

Acquiring the population of participants necessary to have a functioning program can sometimes be as easy as posting information on the bulletin boards at school or it can be more challenging by requiring recruitment. The purpose of the enrichment program will guide the likely student types that will best benefit from the activities. The more diverse the population of participants, the higher the chances of creating transformative learning experiences. Transformative learning experiences can happen to all students and their teachers. When the population of participants in the program is diverse, new experiences assigned from the enrichment activity avail themselves. Some programs are fine-tuned such as computer programming or model boat building. These types of programs target those students interested in the specific activities that coincide with the major topic. The more specific the enrichment program, the narrower the target audience. Broad sweeping experiences touch many diverse learning styles and interests. A thorough understanding of the overall vision and operational vision of an enrichment program will act as guides for the selection of participants.

The vision that guides the overall program is referred to as the overall vision. This vision represents the end goal—the outcome of the overall experience package. The overall vision should inform all participants, staff, stakeholders and interested parties of exactly what the program hopes to achieve. Skills-based programs provide understandable and familiar goals and products. That's not to say that the program shouldn't be innovative and cutting edge. People can recognize even abstract goals and unconventional products. A program that has catapult building and the study of projectile motion as its overarching concepts is not a traditional activity. Yet all parties were able to grasp the concepts necessary to achieve the goals of building a catapult and understanding the motion created by it.

When creating an overall vision, a program director or committee needs to consider this one question and be able to answer it in one or two sentences. "What's the purpose of this program?" The overall vision should be able to sum up the purpose quickly and concisely. An example of this type of vision statement could be as follows, "We are going to build scaled-down catapults and have a competition to see which team's catapult is the most effective. We are going to study the projectile motion created by a catapult and other devices. Topics such as history, physics and mathematics will play a large role in the experience." By having an overall vision, all parties involved in the enrichment program will have a clear understanding of what the purpose is and will be able to notice if the program gets off track.

Once the question of what this program hopes to accomplish has been answered, the next questions that must be answered deal with the day-by-day operations and expectations of a program session. This type of vision can be referred to as operational vision. The operational vision of a program is very similar to a generalized lesson plan or syllabus for a class. The operational vision can differ from session to session in its specifics but it must adhere to the overall format laid out by the operational vision. Consistency is important in many aspects of education, most especially for an enrichment program. A routine such as arriving at the enrichment site and sitting down and having a snack with the members of the program is an example of consistency.

The length of time for various activities and the transition from one activity to another should have a regulated type of function. The mechanics of how the program operates should become second nature to the participants. The information and experiences the program provides should be the center of the participants' attention. The consistency of the operation of the program will help support the learning community necessary for the program to be successful. The program is based on education, therefore, the establishment of a learning community is integral to the program. In the learning community or the program, members all have their roles and sometimes these roles can change.

The individual with the most responsibility to oversee the success of the program and its operations is known as the program director. A program director can be an individual teacher in their own classroom after school or the program director can be in charge of a number of adult staff. With the program director as the overall leader, individual teachers act as both mentors and instructors while other adults can be instructors as well as food service workers as an example. The program director differs from other administrators in the sense that they must be more the host and the servant rather than the commanding general.

When the program director arrives at any part of the activities, there should be an overall feeling of excitement and interest. The program director is the driving force behind the program. They are usually the ones that have the vision and are motivated the most to do the most. The program director arrives first and leaves last. They should be inspiring to both participants and staff. They need to be nonthreatening yet assured and focused. They must be willing to sacrifice above and beyond others for the sake of the success of the program. The program director is not an easy job and sometimes it is thankless but without them, there can be no program. Some may say why would someone want to take on so much responsibility for such minimal compensation? It is the intangible success of the participants and the program that is the true motivation behind the director's energy, enthusiasm and often finances. A program can't operate that well if it requires funding and has none. The program director is usually the number one fundraiser or coordinator of fundraisers.

Money may not be necessary to operate an enrichment program. The program may only require resources that can be provided by parties that possess those resources. One example is the donation by a supporting school principal of archery equipment that was no longer part of the curriculum of the school district. Fundraising is also resource gathering. Programs require resources. Sometimes the program director can purchase those resources or provide resources themselves. When the resources required come with too high a price tag, donations must be acquired. There are many ways donations can be acquired. Simply going to local businesses and presenting your overall vision and operational vision can be enough to gather their support.

Some businesses will donate money while others will donate materials and equipment and still others will donate their time and knowledge. Successful programs have a combination of all funding and resources. Sometimes, student sales can help raise funds. The sales can often compete with other programs that have established sales and times in which the sales occur. The more other programs and activities use student sales as a fundraising method, the harder it is to use again. Creative fundraising may be an alternative for some programs. If the program has the availability of printing t-shirts or getting them donated at a low price, selling those t-shirts can generate the funds necessary to operate the program. Whatever the case, creative fundraising is going to be a constant to assist in the program's longevity. Programs can operate on a shoestring budget. The type of program will dictate the amount of resources and financial assistance required. Understanding how to start each type of program will give a program director the understanding of the resources and funding required.

The simplest type of program to start is one that nearly starts itself. This type of program can be called a grassroots program. Grassroots because it starts with the student's desire to have something enriching occur beyond the school day. Students may approach a teacher or administrator with an idea for a program they would like to have available. Sometimes by just opening up a classroom and having a teacher there, students will gravitate to the space and begin a kind of makeshift program. If students have an interest in a specific hobby, they may need a place for their hobby to occur. Sometimes, the students may just gather because they have nothing to do beyond the school day other than sit in their own house and be bored.

Populating a grassroots program is usually not an issue. The students will have already gathered and all they need is a direction and some supervision. Springboarding off the students' interest, a willing program director can create a goal or product for the group and develop an overall vision. The type of activities the student group would like to do will dictate the number of participants the program can accommodate. Acquiring resources for this type of program can often be as simple as meeting with an administrator or curriculum director and explaining the goals of the enrichment program. A program director can self-fund small inexpensive programs that require time and energy more than resources and money. Grassroots programs can work themselves into more extensive and involved programs the longer the activities can hold the interest of the students involved. Word-of-mouth and friendships often increase the number of participants in these types of programs. School district administration most likely will be receptive to something that is created by student interest and has a motivated adult mentor to supervise the program. Grassroots programs do not have to specifically be started by the students but can be initiated by the program director if an understanding of students' interests and dedication are known.

The semi-structured program is perhaps the least stressful for the program director. It also is easier to start, manage and maintain. The most important aspect that differentiates this type of program from the others is the support from the administration of the school district or organization. By having the support of entities that control insurance, utilities and so on creates an advantage for the more creative program visions. These programs can be initiated by an administrator or a fellow teacher or even a member of the community. If the program director is interested in the concept for the enrichment program, there is already a support system in place. Most programs begin with the program director or classroom teacher. The ideas, needs and the desire of the students to have such a program can inspire an educator to pursue the support of the administration. Curriculum directors are by far the most effective facilitators for these types of programs. Presenting the overall vision and demonstrating a need for the program will work to convince most curriculum directors to support the project. Once the support of the curriculum director is gained, more assets, funding and resources become available. Acquiring the necessary materials to operate the program may be as simple as filling out a supply requisition. Almost every administrative function that is required to operate an extracurricular enrichment program can be handled by individuals that have that as their main function. Principals and other administrators have budgets and materials available. Most school districts already have a process for compensating teachers for work outside the school day. The details of management can be taken care of by freeing up the program director to become their creative and dynamic self.

Some cautionary words at this time may be helpful. Always follow the operating rules of the organization supporting the program. If you're a classroom teacher, the same rules that apply during the school day apply after school. Though a grassroots and semi-structured program can be laxer than a classroom, the need for adherence to general rules and principles as well as accurate attendance are also necessary. If the program takes place after school hours, then the building is most likely near empty. Regardless of how trustworthy honest and reliable students are, they are still young and can make misjudgments. Program directors have to always maintain a safe and well-regulated activity session. When dealing with funding, always be transparent and organized. General pragmatism can guide a program director's managerial style and still maintain individual creativity.

Franchise programs have an existing format that a program director can structure their enrichment activities around. The structure and operating rules for the franchising model program are already in place. A new enrichment program can attach itself to an already existing larger more structured program. A program director or school district can adopt an established program model from a vendor. Another form franchise programs take occurs when a program director joins the staff of a much larger structured program and is allowed to design their own version for a subject discipline. Whichever version is used will come with its own constraints and advantages. Because it is an established program, a program director's vision of their enrichment program will have to conform to an existing structure. The advantages of such an existing structure come when many of the managerial and design issues are already ironed out.

Packaged programs usually come with some workshops, and nowadays, videos and online meetings. The package program is marketed as a complete enrichment experience for students to participate. The advantages of this type of program come from proven success. The rigid adherence to an existing structure may limit the creativity and enthusiasm of the program director. If the program director is the initiator of this package program, the chances of success are greatly increased. Because it is derived from a program of long-standing, the explanation of its vision and goals will have clarity. Recruiting staff will be easier due to its direct support from the school district or other organizations. Some problems that may arise will come from the inexperience of the staff or their reluctance to fully engage in the program. Either one of these can cause a program to fail. Though the packaged program eliminates a lot of the groundwork that must be done to create a truly enriching program, the deep connection with the vision of the program may be harder to convey.

The most complex, time-intensive and labor-intensive is the fully structured program. This program requires a complete ground-up approach for its instruction and operation. For the Ben Franklin School of Industry, I took three months to develop all the print material and gather all the funds and resources necessary to operate a one-week intensive enrichment program. When a program director or committee wants to take on such an enterprise, the end goal and product should be the starting point. This is true for all extracurricular enrichment programs, especially the fully structured program.

Once the goal and product are established, the overall vision can be created. The first program of the Ben Franklin school of industry had a product of a scale model catapult and a goal of utilizing the catapult in a competition. From knowing the product and the goal, a more eloquent operational vision statement can be created, such as, "Students will work in teams to develop skills of construction, design and product management while exploring both the science and the history behind catapults and projectile motion." By developing the overall vision statement from the end goal and product of the program, a director then gains a deeper understanding of how to achieve the most success for the program.

Once the overall vision has been firmed up, the operational vision of each session of the program can be developed. The operational vision is a more loosely designed lesson plan. Depending on the level of intricacy and facilitator involvement, operational visions for each session may be more detailed or remain vague. The amount of preparation can be clearly spelled out or reliant on the knowledge of the facilitator's experience in leading this type of activity. The overall order of activities can be standardized or differ from session to session. A fully structured program may have component enrichment activities, and upon the completion of the activity, there should be a smooth transition to the next activity. Understanding the broader scope of what is to be accomplished by the program will assist in the development of the smooth and efficient movement of students. If the students stay in the same location and only the instructor changes, there will still be transition time required. For static location programs, the transition can be a mini activity. The closer it ties the previous activity to the new activity, the more valuable the transition period becomes.

A fully structured program benefits from a thoroughly developed methodology, the definition of rules and an outline of the various roles of the staff and students. Clear expectations of behavior and attendance must be established in order to ensure the longevity of the program. It is highly recommended that a program director develops a handbook that clearly presents all the program expectations and functions. The handbook should include the various types of activities and the skills that these activities introduce or enhance. A brochure that quickly presents the overall vision and operational vision will aid in recruiting both staff and students as well as stakeholders to the program. More so than any other program, an information sheet and parents' permission sheet should be developed and distributed and filed. The more physical the activity, the more precautions must be taken, such as liability sheets where the parent grants some latitude to the program and its staff regarding events that were beyond the program's control. The school of industry utilized power tools for construction. By having an industrial arts instructor on staff and a safety officer, liabilities were reduced. A safety officer is just a staff member that has training in overall safety. Nurses and EMTs are examples of perfect candidates for the role of safety officer. Protecting the program and its participants is another one of the responsibilities of a program director.

For enrichment programs that take place in the off-season of school or consistently for a time and cover an expansive area such as several floors of the school or both an indoor and outdoor environment, the program director will need good walking shoes. The program director must constantly circulate through-out the locations of the program activities. The leadership dem-onstrated by the program director will differ from the leadership demonstrated by other school administrations. As the program director, he or she chooses staff members wisely and trusts in their ability to execute their assignments to the best of their abil-ity. By choosing very accomplished staff members or younger staff members willing to be mentored, the program director can have confidence that the only supervision necessary of staff is to assist in accomplishing their assigned activity.

Once a program director arrives at a site for an enrichment activity, smiles and warm welcomes should be commonplace from staff and students. The program director is there to see to the needs of the program and must be ready for a constant influx of requests for resources or solutions to dilemmas. The program director is truly the deciding individual when staff and students cannot solve a specific problem. Once the problem is identified, it's up to the program director to gather the resources or allocate the funds that will rectify the situation. Program directors do not utilize formal observations as a method of determination of the staff's capabilities and effectiveness. Because the choice of com-petent staff was made at the very beginning of the program, it is unnecessary for a program director to supervise the staff in the same manner as a principal would supervise the teaching staff. Because of the change of attitude of administration from one of superiority and authority to one of cooperation and assistance, current school administrators will find it a little more difficult to develop a community atmosphere that is conducive to program success. This is not to say that current administrators can't do this job, it is merely a reminder of how difficult it can be when the lines between friendship and authority are blurred in such a manner.

The more encompassing the program's goals and products are, the more need for well-defined operational procedures. This again stresses the need for documentation and starts to clearly define the responsibilities of the program director and what responsibilities can be delegated to staff. Extracurricular activities must take into account the necessity for nourishment.

Time to eat must be accommodated and utilized as a community-building activity. Food needs to be prepared ahead of time. Often, program directors are teaching at their regular position during the time the food needs to be prepared. Competent staff that can handle the nutrition aspect and serve the food to the participants will ease the burden on a program director. Optimally, the enrichment program should have an individual in charge of nutrition and food services that is separate from the program director.

Attendance will be a very important part of every program, therefore, someone in charge of attendance is necessary. Having interns or volunteers with specific duties to take attendance will increase the efficiency of the program. By clearly defining the roles of the instructor, the staff members in charge of mentoring and conveying educational information and skills will have prior knowledge of their expectations. Projects and goals that require student teams and educator teams to accomplish the goals help create a highly impacting learning community. When a problem facing the students is also a problem facing the instructors, such as the construction of a catapult, all participants see how cooperation and sharing of knowledge contribute to the success of the activity. A thorough knowledge of each student participant enables the program director and staff to address individual needs prior to difficulties arising. Awareness of health issues and food allergies is very important knowledge that assists in meeting the needs of all participants.

Developing a fully structured program is demanding on many levels and should not be pursued without prior experience in enrichment programs and other community activities. Organizations and schools that wish to develop fully structured extracurricular enrichment programs may find that a semi-structured program is more manageable, which can then be evolved into a fully structured program. An initiative to change the entire educational structure of a middle school may take half a year to develop before it can be implemented. When my district pursued a restructuring of its middle school education model, four master teachers were selected and given the directive to develop a cohort-based schoolwide system. These four teachers developed a project that would bring teams of students throughout the grade levels together and focus them on the goal of the overall project. Because the district's emphasis was on building learning communities, the product selected was known as a community project. Students in small groups would develop an entire plan for an imaginary community. Each group had to include aspects of all subjects taught at the middle school level.

This multidisciplinary approach provided outside classroom experiences in all the various subjects. Standard fundamental skills were utilized to create an enriching product, which was a brochure and handbook detailing all aspects of the community the students had developed. The district incorporated the community project as the vehicle to transform a single subject system of educating students into a cohort-centered multidisciplinary system. Primarily, an extracurricular enrichment program needs to be transformative in its overall nature. Those that participate in such a program should have increased knowledge and skills as well as a sense of accomplishment.

The importance of enrichment programs cannot be overstated. The fundamentals are like building a house; it is the enrichment program that adds the appliances, the furniture and the paint on the walls, all the things that make a building a home. It is difficult to tell which enrichment program will benefit the most students. Having a variety of enrichment choices from which students can pick and choose the direction in which they want to go is the most advantageous to learning. If a program only reaches a small number of students, that is still better than never having reached any students. The enrichment program may well be the most significant educational experience a student has. The parable of the starfish might be fitting to bring this book to its conclusion.

In the early morning, a beach has two people on it. One person is standing watching the other. The other person is moving down the beach, picking up starfish that have washed ashore and throwing them back into the water. The observer asks the person throwing the starfish back into the ocean, "why bother?" The observer continues, "the shore is littered with thousands of starfish what difference does it make throwing one back into the ocean?" The other person responds, "it made a difference to this starfish," as the person throws the starfish back into the ocean. The story usually ends here, reminding us that even one child saved makes a difference. I carry the story a little further. The observer now joins the original person and starts picking up starfish and throwing them back into the ocean. When the two of them get to the end of the beach, they turn around and see that hundreds of people have followed behind them, each of them throwing starfish into the ocean. If we all try to enrich our students and create programs that will help them develop the skills of self-confidence and new knowledge, we will make a difference in a multitude of lives.